101 WAYS YOUR CHURCH CAN CHANGE THE WORLD

TONY CAMPOLO

A Guide

to Help

Christians

Express

the Love

of Christ

to a Needy

World

GORDON AESCHLIMAN

Regal Books
A Division of Gospel Light
Ventura, California, U.S.A.

Published by Regal Books
A Division of Gospel Light
Ventura, California, U.S.A.
Printed in U.S.A.

Regal Books is a ministry of Gospel Light, an evangelical Christian publisher dedicated to serving the local church. We believe God's vision for Gospel Light is to provide church leaders with biblical, user-friendly materials that will help them evangelize, disciple and minister to children, youth and families.

It is our prayer that this Regal Book will help you discover biblical truth for your own life and help you meet the needs of others. May God richly bless you.

For a free catalog of resources from Regal Books/Gospel Light please contact your Christian supplier or call 1-800-4-GOSPEL.

Library of Congress Cataloging-in-Publication Data
Campolo, Anthony.
    101 ways your church can change the world : a guide to help
  Christians express the love of Christ to a needy world / Tony
  Campolo, Gordon Aeschliman.
      p. cm.
    ISBN 0-8307-1650-5 (hard cover)
    1. Pastoral theology. 2. Church renewal—United States.
  I. Aeschliman, Gordon D., 1957-   . II. Title. III. Title: One hundred and
  one ways your church can change the world.
  BV4011.C35 1993
  253—dc20
                                                                93-37347
                                                                    CIP

Rights for publishing this book in other languages are contracted by Gospel Literature International (GLINT). GLINT also provides technical help for the adaptation, translation and publishing of Bible study resources and books in scores of languages worldwide. For further information, contact GLINT, P.O. Box 4060, Ontario, CA 91761-1003, U.S.A., or the publisher.

CONTENTS

INTRODUCTION

This book is about being Christian—living out the good news. We believe that there is nothing better for the world than a vibrant fellowship of people who have fallen in love with Jesus and who daily follow Him into the pain of society.

As we have crisscrossed the nation, we have been refreshed in our own faith by the quiet but forceful lifestyle of thousands of congregations that are going about the business of their Lord. No flashy programs or expansive buildings. No large budgets and very little public recognition. No powerful base to influence the political brokers of the capitol. No TV networks or radio stations to broadcast their views. Their work and influence are much more potent than all of these.

What we are witnessing is a quiet revolution of love—people who are captured by the call of Calvary and who resolve to be the incarnated hands, feet and arms of Jesus. They may not be celebrities in the world's eyes (nor the church's for that matter), but the angels sing their praise in heaven.

We are impressed by the leaders of these congregations and fellowships. Our times are not that far removed from the era of confused Christian leadership—those days when "leadership" was a pompous "I'm-in-charge" style that looked very little like the Lamb who stood silent before accusers and then painfully bled to death on a rough-hewn cross. These true church leaders are not dictatorial or power hungry, neither are they shaped by the contemporary wisdom of what it means to be a "Christian leader." They are not so visible. They are not asserting their authority over others. They are not enlarging their spheres of control. They are not "telling" others how they ought to live their lives. They are not distinguishing themselves by drawing battle lines on obscure doctrine.

No, the lives of these Christian leaders are much more noble. Their doctrine is mostly the visible love of Jesus in action. They live in the mess of society, at the crossroads of pain and evil. They are like the prophets who cannot preach about suffering without first crying tears of genuine brokenness for the "least of these" (Matt. 25:40,45). These men and women are not building a kingdom made of mortar, pews and ratings. They are building the kingdom of Jesus, and it looks a lot like a company of the sick, the orphan, the widow, the prostitute and the tax collector. Their sanctuary is the foot of the Cross and their prayer is, "Jesus, please be merciful to me, a sinner."

These leaders are carried by a firm and unshakeable peace that comes from heaven. They have experienced how deep is the love of Jesus that surpasses all knowledge. Their significance is measured by that love, and they are secure in it. They are not ashamed of Jesus, nor are they looking to be well spoken of by others. Their ministry is rooted in the personal experience of God's grace, and the gimmicks of this world are no match for so great a gift. The people they lead are marked by the force of the golden rule: to love their neighbors as themselves. This honest measure of leadership is the kind for which the world longs.

And the world longs for the depth of their love. These leaders have not met the Jesus who cares only about a person's soul, without regard for physical and emotional needs. They have walked with the Lord who grieves with the widow, visits the prisoner, heals the sick, clothes the naked, gives dignity to the disabled and sets the oppressed free.

The integrity of their doctrine is measured by the breadth of human pain they touch. May God increase their numbers!

We have an agenda in writing this book. We believe that society has been let down too often by a church that does not reflect the deep, powerful and wholesome love of our Jesus. We believe that the Church often lacks the creativity and courage the gospel demands of us, so it chooses the lower road—it mimics the ways of society. This book is for everyone in God's Church who is committed to taking Jesus' love to a hurting world: pastors, church staff, lay leaders and all concerned Christians willing to "stand in the gap."

In this book, we are offering a broad range of ideas and resources that come from the trenches. They have been tried by people who bear the scars of society's pain, people who do not consider "advancement" a promotion to higher status, but rather the privilege to go deeper into the human dilemma. We are not elevating any person or congregation in this book. That would go against the spirit of what we are trying to accomplish. We hope you will find this a friendly resource, a sort of desk manual for helping your congregation impact society.

The book is broken into 13 sections: evangelism, the poor, youth, missions, the environment, the sick, prisoners, the elderly, the immigrant, the family, the oppressed, the handicapped and life. Each section features an introduction to the topic being addressed, followed by an array of practical ideas. Near the end of each section is a "Spread the Vision" segment, which provides ideas to generate enthusiasm among your congregation. Additional recommended resources for your interest and inspiration close each section. At the end of the book, we have designed a 13-week Sunday School curriculum. Each of the weekly lessons follows the themes of this resource manual.

We have designed this book as an introduction to the biblical call to touch all the world with the good news of

Jesus Christ, and we hope you will find practical, useful ideas as your church seeks to reach society. We pray you will experience the fullness of God's blessing in the days ahead as you lead your fellow workers in the path of God's love.

I.
EVANGELISM
Proclaiming the Good News

Have you ever wondered why cold-turkey evangelism feels so unnatural? It is awkward to approach complete strangers and try to tell them in a few minutes, using the help of a survey or booklet, that their life is off track and needs to be turned over to Jesus.

The reason it feels unnatural is because it *is* unnatural!

If you feel uncomfortable about this tact, it is for a good reason. God never intended for evangelism to be a mini sales presentation. We are not competing for people's minds and hearts in the smorgasbord of world religions; neither are we attempting to convince unbelieving people with debate and argument. Evangelism should feel as natural as breathing. In fact, we assert that sharing our faith is *spiritual breathing*. All props aside, evangelism is that normal exchange we have with our surroundings. We take in, and we give out. And not surprisingly, it is this exchange that keeps us spiritually alive.

The Church in North America has largely failed in our evangelism efforts. This is a curious fact when you consider the billions of dollars we spend on outreach programs each year—building projects, radio, TV, literature, training seminars and crusades. Yet our society simply does not have the stamp of the Holy Spirit upon it. If all our programs led to spiritual life, we would not see such rampant deceit, violence, pornography, racism and other forms of injustice.

If the Church were more effective, we would see a society that reflects the fruit of the Holy Spirit: love, joy, peace, patience, kindness, goodness, faithfulness, gentleness and self-control (Gal. 5:22,23). And in a purely pragmatic measuring, we would see churches bursting with people who have traditionally found no home in the church. However, most of the large congregations are made up of people who have "moved over" from another fellowship. At the national level, our total church population is not even keeping pace with the growth rate of the general population.

We don't think it makes sense to harangue our church members into evangelistic programs any more than it does to beat the general population over the head and scream, "You must breathe, you idiots!" Our evangelism—our breathing, if you will—is living the life of a Spirit-filled Christian *in the presence of people outside the family of faith.* Too often we are trained to bombard people with our beliefs. We rush into their world with our doctrinal message and then escape to the safety of our churches once we have dispensed the package.

But evangelism is not a spiritual raid on the enemy. Rather than "invade enemy territory" or "execute surgical strikes," we are called to *live among* people who have not found the love of Jesus. Our life of love, tenderness and righteousness becomes the bridge by which the Holy Spirit woos them into the kingdom of God. No gimmicks here. We are talking about the demanding work of developing friendships with people who have not yet discovered that God is truly their friend. This may sound rather simplistic, but then Jesus said, "Let the little children come to me, and do not hinder them, for the kingdom of heaven belongs to such as these" (Matt. 19:14).

A song many of us learned in Sunday School says: "This world is not my home, I'm just a-passin' through. My treasures are laid up, somewhere beyond the blue. The angels beckon me from heaven's open door, and I can't feel at home in this world anymore." A great song, but it is only half true! Christians must live in the tension of *not* being at home while at the same time being at home.

This world is half our home. Christ has put us here to plant our roots deep in the soil of contemporary society By

-filled living, we enlarge the influence of
. demonstrate God's love to the world.
old not to be "of the world," we are called
ld. Maybe our traditional evangelistic pro-
grams serve as a trade-off: We like the security of the church,
but we feel we ought to do something about the people "out
there." So we design ways to temporarily "be in the world."

But we cannot temporarily breathe.

Pastors and lay leaders need to guide their churches
back into society. They need to think of the places where
the gospel is absent and then pray for the courage and
grace to live out their Christianity in that context. Their fellowships will model that same kind of lifestyle. Nothing
could be more natural for a Christian.

Hopefully, as we become the presence of Jesus in society, we will be able to add those few words and warm
hugs that help people make the final step into the arms of
Jesus. This is evangelism at its best.

1. Leave the Church

This idea could be a bit threatening to people whose pro-
fession is to call others *into* the Church. But we are serious about this evangelistic notion.

We suggest that pastors and lay leaders start by looking
at their weekly routines. How much of the week is spent in
the natural environment of people outside of the faith?
Some pastors and other church staff may say, "I'm paid to
care for the flock." True, but that is not a good enough reason to avoid contact with the world. Pastors may need to
help their churches (or more specifically, their elders or
deacons) to understand that one cannot be a minister in
good faith and live separate from society. Lay leaders, as
well, who are not employed by the church, often find that
much of their time is spent planning activities or attending

board meetings. This type of service is good and necessary, but the danger comes when it prevents building relationships outside of the church.

Yes, church work is highly demanding of our time. But society is more demanding. We need to consciously leave the security of fellow believers and put ourselves in an environment where Christ intends the Church to live. Here are several ways to make the step:

- Think of groups that are typically unlike your regular circle of friends. Perhaps they have different political views or are part of a vocation that is unfamiliar to you. Find out where they gather, and begin to attend their events. Learn about their beliefs and activities. Listen to their needs and aspirations. Pray for sensitivity to their way of viewing life. Volunteer to help them with projects that do not directly conflict with your values.

- If you enjoy sports, join a local club. Surround yourself with people you do not know, and pray for the opportunity to meet people outside of the faith. Pray for them to become regular sports partners and genuine friends.

- Open your home to neighbors. In the summer, invite them over for barbecues. On special national occasions—Fourth of July, Thanksgiving, Mother's Day—host parties for them in your home.

- Join local societies or service organizations that fit your interests—sports, chorale, arts, Toastmasters, PTA, Lions Club, Big Brothers-

Big Sisters—and look for opportunities to
build friendships with people who do not
know Jesus.

You could add several more to the list. In all of these
endeavors, strive to develop genuine friendships. It is not
necessary to jump into an unnatural "evangelistic" relationship. In time, God will allow your life to become sweet
aroma, water to a thirsty heart. Let that be a natural process
guided by the work of the Holy Spirit; with His guidance,
it will be clear when and how to add words to your lifestyle.

One other thought: It is tempting to think that people
who have different beliefs do not know Jesus. This could be
nothing more than a form of spiritual prejudice. We encourage you to surround yourself with people whose views
appear to conflict with your own. There are at least two
good reasons for this: you may be surprised to see how
much they love Jesus, and you will gain a more honest
view of the "other side."

2. Send Your Congregation Away

We are serious. Tell your congregation to quit hanging
around the church.

So much of the teaching today leads people to think that
their Christianity is best lived out by volunteering all of
their spare hours to church functions. In fact, we have
become very sophisticated in our ability to convince people that God will be especially pleased with them if they
would just get with the church program.

Too many churchgoers look like they were caught in the
spin cycle of a commercial washing machine, and unfortunately, they think they are doing it for Jesus. Teach Sunday
School, help in the nursery, clean the sanctuary, sit on this
board or that committee, pour punch, hand out leaflets,
attend this seminar, join the prayer group and attend regu-

lar services. Each of these, by themselves, may hold value for the churchgoer and may be a genuine service. But with so many demands and expectations, the message is that good Christians pour all of their nonworking hours into programs that take them away from their neighborhoods and communities. And the more haggard they look, the more spiritual they are. This is heresy. Jesus said, "Go into all the world and preach the good news to all creation" (Mark 16:15). Clearly, He meant for us to mingle among those outside of the faith and be a light amidst the darkness.

We think pastors should suggest that their parishioners spend at least half of their volunteer hours *outside of the church family*. Add it up: Sunday service, prayer meeting, Bible study, choir, youth group, board meeting, committee meetings, fellowship evenings, outreach programs (still a "church thing"). Maybe we are all spending 10 or 15 hours a week at some kind of church-sponsored event. It is great for a pastor to have such a devoted congregation. People who regularly volunteer their time and energy are often the backbone of the church; they keep things running and take up the slack for an overworked church staff. But it is likely that some people devote too much time to the church and end up with unbalanced lives.

So if 10 hours are normally spent at church each week, we suggest pastors ask people to spend 5 of those hours at something completely unrelated to official church events. This should be a clear and clarion call. The leaders should work to convince their members that the church cannot be successful if they do not rub shoulders with those who don't know Jesus.

We also recommend that you be as specific as possible in offering ideas for leaving the church. If some members are already doing this, let them tell their story to the rest of the congregation. Clearly, we are suggesting a notion that could be threatening to some pastors—asking their members to volunteer *less* for church activities. But we believe it is dishonest to call people into a deeper relationship with Christ if the way to do that is by leaving the world completely (see John 17:15). Jesus left His home and came into the world. He was ridiculed by the religious leaders of His day for hanging around with the "publicans, prostitutes and tax collectors" (see Matt. 9:11 and Matt. 11:19). What they did not understand was that their accusations were affirming His credentials. And we are to follow the example of Christ, who instructs us, "As the Father has sent me, I am sending you" (John 20:21).

Actually, we do not think churches will get emptier if pastors keep sending out their members; they will get *fuller.* These members will be free to mix with people outside the church. These encounters will naturally lead to evangelistic opportunities and then pastors will be saddled with the wonderful problem of new members who are hungry to grow in Christ.

3. Practice Hospitality

Imagine hardened leaders of a labor union meeting for prayer and Bible study in the basement of a church. It happened recently in New York.

A friend of ours ministers at a church that is located across the street from a business that was recently the target of a strike. Every day the organized workers walked up and down the sidewalk with placards bearing messages of unfair labor contracts. Some mean tactics were being used against those employees who crossed the picket lines, and church and civil leaders (our friend included) condemned the malicious behavior of the strike leaders.

The strike lasted into the winter, and on a bitterly cold New York morning, the Lord prompted this pastor to provide a place of warmth for the strikers.

He must have thought, *You've got to be kidding, Lord!*
Nope.

He set up a coffee table in the church basement and
went over to the very people he had condemned, inviting
them to use the church—coffee and all—as needed to take
shelter from the cold. The invitation was enthusiastically
received, and soon the church became a regular place of
relief and relaxation. Church staff began to mix with the
strikers, and before long, prejudices began to slip away as
real men and women replaced the caricature of hardened
labor leaders.

The strike lasted the entire winter, and our pastor-friend
thinks that was part of God's strategy. All of the unstruc-
tured downtime allowed for hearty arguments about life
and religion. Halfway into the winter, several strikers joined
the pastor for a special Bible study each morning. The pastor was able to pray with these people who were experiencing the economic crunch of the strike. Church staff visited family members who were sick, and some of the families became regular church attenders. By the time the strike
ended, several of these people had given their lives to Christ.

What went on here? The church was willing to follow
Jesus' words, "Love your enemies, do good to them, and lend
to them without expecting to get anything back" (Luke 6:35).
We would naturally provide shelter for our friends; Jesus
wants us to do the same for those we do not call "friend."
This sort of hospitality is at the heart of what it means to be
a Christian and easily paves a way to Christ. This pastor was
responding to the Lord's nudges. The genuine nature of his
deeds spoke clearly regarding the substance of the gospel
and in addition paved the way for evangelism.

A church can provide hospitality in many ways—for no
other reason than caring about people. The world does not
experience enough of this no-strings-attached love. We suggest that you think through ways to be hospitable to the

local community. Involve church members who have gifts in this area. Here are a few suggestions:

- Hold an annual appreciation banquet for community leaders who take exceptional steps to serve the local citizens.

- Host a similar event for volunteer staff of local shelters, children's homes, tutoring programs and clinics. Coordinate with the leaders of these groups. State up front that your singular agenda is to show appreciation for their service. If there is suspicion regarding your motives, hold the banquet in a local school.

- Offer a quarterly "Get to Know Your City" dessert for people who are new to the neighborhood. Bring in local officials—school principals, the fire chief, the police chief, librarian, parks and recreation staff, representatives from the chamber of commerce—to acquaint the newcomers to all the services of the town.

These simple acts of love cut across the hurried and often harsh pace of life. The message "we love you" is all too scarce, and who but the family of God should be there to say it?

4. Model Unity

The Church is terribly splintered and fragmented. So many denominations, so many factions. A wide variety of doctrinal beliefs, bylaws and leadership structures. Churches located next door to each other may not ever intermingle. That is sad—and damaging.

Unity is scary to many of us. Perhaps we are wary of those with different doctrinal beliefs. Maybe we are comfortable in our own traditions and rituals, and we do not want anyone to "rock the boat." Or maybe we derive security from our subtle prejudices (they tell us we are "okay" in contrast to others). All of these things can hinder the bond of unity believers can share. But when we get close to other Christians, we often discover that our prejudices against them are unkind and untrue.

Jesus preached unity as one of the two principal means people would be able to recognize God. (The other is love.) Unity is perhaps the clearest road to honesty: We end up believing the best (and the truth) about each other. And we *tell* the truth about each other. God hates malicious talk so much that it is equated with ignoring the hungry (see Isa. 58:4-7,9,10).

In Jesus' great prayer of John 17, He asks the Father to bring unity among the disciples in the same way that Jesus and the Father are unified. This, says Jesus, will be a testimony to the world and will give people the power to believe.

It is our conviction that the lack of unity in the Church today is a chief reason the world cannot see Jesus. This book is written to leaders, and so in that context we appeal to those in authority to understand the high calling of unity. Few of Jesus' prayers were recorded, but the Holy Spirit must have had reasons to make sure His unity prayer made its way into the final text. The unity expressed by the Trinity is illustrated as well in the inspiration of the Scriptures. In John 1:1 we read the mystical notion: "In the beginning was the Word, and the Word was with God, and the Word was God."

As leaders, we cannot feel free to go about the work of ministry if we are causing divisions in the Body. We would not be following Christ's way (see Eph. 4:1-3; Phil. 2:1-3). We would be putting stumbling blocks in the way of the world and in fact would be shutting heaven's door on people for whom the blood of Calvary was shed.

We have several suggestions on how to begin building unity:

- Establish an exchange program with local pastors, taking turns in each other's pulpits. It would be great if once a month your pulpit was filled by a local visiting pastor.

- Plan a few annual events that bring together several local churches in a unified program.

- Offer services to the public that are sponsored by a consortium of churches. Make it clear that these are not just offered by one denomination.

- Encourage your church members to visit other congregations from time to time. Advertise special events being offered by other churches.

- Every so often, preach a series on what doctrinal positions are similar between local congregations (we already hear enough about the differences).

We simply cannot underestimate the power of unity (see Ps. 133:1,3). As we begin to live a unified lifestyle among ourselves, we will develop a warm and inviting spirit that cuts across the pattern of a world that is torn by hostility, mistrust, ethnic strife, racism, sexism and extreme nationalism. Protestants are killing Catholics, Catholics are killing Protestants, Christians are killing Muslims, Muslims are killing Christians, Muslims are killing Muslims. We need to minister to the world in the opposite spirit. We need to show that in Christ there is a true love that tears down barriers, a love that brings together a wonderful collection of tribes, tongues and nations. Among God's people there is peace instead of strife. We need to pray that God will give us a deep desire to love one another as we love ourselves. And then we need to act on it.

During the confusing and hurtful months that followed the riots of Los Angeles in 1992, churches of various denominations and persuasions came together and asked God to forgive them for their sin of division and strife. They asked the Lord to teach them to love one another as Christ loved them. Several of these encounters were captured by the news media, and some newscasters fell silent at the end of those reports. God is giving us the opportunity to live in unity and so bear testimony to the world. Let us not miss this critical time in our history to be good witnesses for our Lord.

5. Go Tell the News

We are blessed with several good organizations that can help us take new steps in the direction of evangelism. It makes a lot of sense for pastors and leaders to ask these ministries to help them grow in their understanding of evangelism.

We recommend that congregations make a minimal commitment to evangelism-on-the-road. The goal could be as simple as, "We want 10 of our adults and 15 of our youth to go on an evangelism trip each year."

We must be careful that we do not fall into the trap of doing evangelism "out there" if we are unable to commit ourselves to the idea locally. But having said that, evangelism trips can serve as an excellent opportunity to sharpen our commitment, gain courage and experience God's faithfulness. We regularly hear stories of people who come back from these trips with a new energy. They return revitalized. Perhaps their hearts have been given a jump start, and they recognize the true nature of their faith. Here are some basic ideas for taking it on the road:

- If you live in a large urban area, ask around about ministries that are located in the inner

city. Arrange for weekend plunges where you
become a partner with someone who lives
there full time. Your members will begin to
feel the excitement of living in expectation that
God will touch others through them.

- Link up for an entire summer with an inner-
  city ministry. Several organizations look for
  Christians who want to serve as short-term
  apprentice evangelists.

- Join a ministry for the summer that uses
  special skills such as drama, music and the arts
  for evangelism. These organizations will take
  you to another country where people speak
  your language but where the distance from
  home puts you into a daily routine of trusting
  the Lord to use you effectively. We know a
  church that has committed itself to pay the
  entire cost for any of its youth who volunteer
  to go on such a trip for the first time. This
  church understands that it is building toward
  the future.

Jesus sent all of His disciples on short-term evangelism
trips. If it worked for the Master, it can work for us, too.

6. Share the Wealth

An annual budget says a lot about a church's priorities.
Unfortunately, too many budgets indicate that programs
"operated and owned" by the church are all that count.
Failing to reach out, many churches become ingrown, focusing only on their own programs and structures.

Our suggestion for giving financially to the ministry of
evangelism is to allocate a certain percentage of the annu-

al budget to evangelistic efforts completely outside of your own programs. This provides a dose of discipline to ensure that evangelism is recognized and supported in other regions and countries.

One helpful mechanism for this is the tithe. Pastors do not often look forward to the annual reminder to members that tithing was God's idea to support the work of the clergy. People naturally mistrust the notion of tithing for two reasons: It is like asking the wolf to establish the rules for the sheep (the pastor is the one benefiting from the rules), and too many real crooks have exploited the biblical notion of stewardship for self-gain. (Of course, the crooks are the rare exception to the vast majority of honest pastors who handle their finances with integrity.)

Carefully research good evangelism options. Involve the church members. Explain that you need their help to identify those key ministries that will receive 10 percent of the annual budget. Members will appreciate the opportunity to lend guidance, and they are more likely to be faithful in their own stewardship if they help decide where the church resources ought to go. And church members bring their own judgment and creativity to this process. The church's giving is enriched by the diverse opportunities that emerge—opportunities that were outside the scope of the pastoral team.

Each month, the church could send out the full 10 percent of collected funds. This could be a time of celebration, as a member reports how much money is being sent and where it is going. If the ministry is local, a representative could be brought in for an update on their program at the same time the funds are handed over.

This sort of regular tithing by the church becomes an integrity check—we give beyond ourselves although we face a budget crunch and feel the need to keep those precious dollars. We model the spirit of giving rather than merely preach about the notion. The message becomes, "Do as I do, not as I say." Parents often teach their children the need to look beyond themselves. Selfishness, we tell them, is like a disease that slowly strangles the soul. How true that is! The church that only preaches giving is suspect and suffocating. The church that cheerfully gives beyond itself is well and alive.

7. Spread the Vision for Evangelism

Choose a date on the church calendar for Evangelism Sunday. This is an opportunity to rehearse the call to evangelism and to celebrate the various ways the church has involved itself in proclaiming the good news during the previous year. Here are a few suggestions for the special Sunday:

- Ask all Sunday School teachers to tie in that week's lesson to the call to evangelism.

- Organize that Sunday's service around the subject of evangelism. Try for something surprising and uplifting. Do not depress the congregation with too many "oughts."

- Have special Bible readings during the service, from both the Old and New Testaments, that illustrate God's unending love for all people.

- Ask members to break into small groups during part of the service to share with others how they came to Christ.

- Create a bulletin insert that describes the various ways the church supported evangelism during the past year.

- If any church members went on evangelistic trips during the year, have them tell the entire congregation about their adventure of faith.

- Invite some local evangelistic ministries to give a special presentation during the service.

- Offer a special Saturday or Sunday afternoon seminar on evangelism for those who want to learn more.

8. Resources for Evangelism

We recommend the following key resources for further growth and involvement in evangelism. In addition, we urge you to take advantage of secular publications that describe the world as it is today. These give insight and background on contemporary society, which makes for much better evangelism.

ORGANIZATIONS

BARNA RESEARCH GROUP, LTD.

P.O. Box 4152
Glendale, CA 91222
Headed by George Barna, this organization researches contemporary society and the church's response to it. Barna publishes *Ministry Currents,* a quarterly newsletter on trends in the church (and two important books by Barna are listed below).

CONCERTS OF PRAYER

P.O. Box 36008
Minneapolis, MN 55435
This group will help you establish a regular public prayer meeting in association with other local churches and ministries.

INTERVARSITY CHRISTIAN FELLOWSHIP
P.O. Box 7895
Madison, WI 53707
This group will help you with
campus evangelism.

JEWS FOR JESUS
60 Haight St.
San Francisco, CA 94102
This organization equips
Christians for Jewish evangelism.

YOUTH WITH A MISSION
P.O. Box 406
Mountain Center, CA 92561
This ministry is able to accommodate
all kinds of groups for short-term
ministry. They also have a special
"Small Half" outreach that involves
children in evangelism.

BOOKS

Fifty Ways You Can Share Your Faith
by Tony Campolo and
Gordon Aeschliman
(InterVarsity, 1993).
The Frog in the Kettle by
George Barna (Regal, 1990).
Out of the Salt Shaker by Becky
Pippert (InterVarsity, 1979).
Reinventing Our Evangelism by Don
Posterski (InterVarsity, 1989).
The Barna Report by George Barna
(Regal), an annual book on the state
of religion in the United States.

VIDEO

The Search
2100 Productions
P.O. Box 7895
Madison, WI 53707
A good video on the
New Age movement.

II.
THE POOR
Lending a Helping Hand

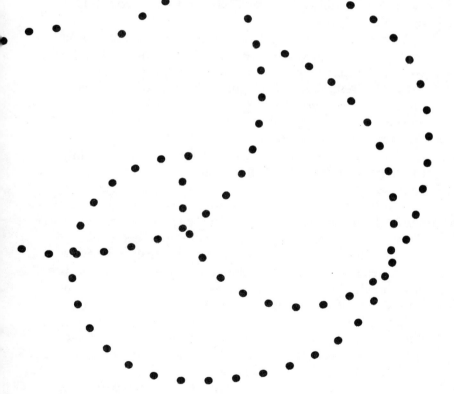

When Jesus walked the earth, He demonstrated a special love and concern for those who were disadvantaged and pressed down by the harsh realities of living. He had compassion for the underprivileged and deprived: "I tell you the truth, whatever you did for one of the least of these brothers of mine, you did for me" (Matt. 25:40).

He never approached the poor as some kind of project or problem that had to be rectified. He genuinely felt the weight of their plight. This should not surprise us, because in the Old Testament, God regularly measured Israel's faithfulness by the degree to which they cared for the poor. To ignore the poor was a direct offense against Yahweh.

There have been times when North American theologians and pastors were confused about their responsibility to the poor. "Evangelism is the great and singular priority," we would hear. The fear was that if Christians became too involved in the physical dimension, they might lose their spiritual orientation and forsake the evangelism mandate. They would be too busy feeding mouths to feed souls.

This temporary departure from the full call of the Scriptures is an unfortunate blip on the screen of the modern Church. We do not have the permission to forsake any dimension of our calling—including care for the poor. Indeed, the Church hurt its witness by inviting the criticism that Christianity has no earthly value. People would say, "Christians do nothing to make the earth a better place; they're only concerned about what lies *beyond* this life. That's pie in the sky." Unfortunately, many times they were

right. That form of "Christianity"—which ignores the immediate needs of our fellow man—has no value to the world.
Besides, that line of thinking certainly is not biblical.

Thank God those days are largely behind us. Yes, a few
groups are "holding out" for a truncated version of the
gospel, but they do not reflect the spirit of the larger
Church. The gospel is indeed good news for the poor, and
we can preach the evangelistic message with integrity
because we know that the Lord of our souls looks com-
passionately upon our physical suffering as well. If a child
asks an earthly parent for bread, he or she will not be given
a stone (see Matt. 7:9-11). How much more can we expect
from our perfect "heavenly Parent"?

Who are the poor today? They are the hungry, homeless, unemployed and impoverished; they are always living on the verge of destruction. A single negative event,
added to their current burdensome plight, can render them
absolutely desolate. We see them on our TV screens in
Somalia—literally millions of men, women and children
just days away from death by starvation. We see them in
Bosnia—victims of wars they did not create nor desire,
homeless and without adequate medical attention for their
wounds. We see them in the rural communities and urban
centers of America—unemployed, malnourished, unedu-
cated and unable to get medical care (perhaps as many as
35 million people). Throughout the world, as many as 1
billion people may be living on the edge of survival. That
is 1 in every 5 human beings.

Clearly, Christians who love and obey Jesus are stirred by
these facts. They do not cling to their wealth and attempt to
justify their lifestyles. Rather, they ask, "What can I do?"
And this question does not spring from a superior attitude
that denigrates those who live in poverty. These Christians
understand that it is the Lord who gives us breath to live
and all other gifts. "There but by the grace of God go I."

Caring for the poor, then, is not some kind of charity we dispense at a distance. No, as followers of Christ, we feel their pain intensely. We cannot live separate from their dilemma any more than we can ignore the pain of our own brother or sister.

Caring for the poor requires looking for long-term solutions to people's circumstances while attempting to alleviate their immediate pain. It means reaching out to people just like us who need a helping hand—our *equals* who do not experience the bounty we have been graced to receive. It means putting aside our prejudices toward the poor and homeless, and receiving them into our lives the same way the King of heaven received us.

The world cannot argue with a Church that lives in the pain of society's poor. The integrity of this form of Christianity silences the harshest of critics, because they know genuine love and compassion when they see it. And the truth is, they want it.

9. Help Habitat for Humanity

A businessman in Americus, Georgia, had this simple idea: No more shacks. As a Christian, it was his opinion that God has compassion on the homeless and that all of God's children should have adequate shelter to provide warmth, safety, privacy and sanctuary.

He created a ministry called Habitat for Humanity, which today has the hands-on construction help of such notables as former President Jimmy Carter and Watergate celebrity Chuck Colson. More than 25,000 homes have been built for the poor, and the program is attracting more and more volunteers all the time.

Here is how Habitat for Humanity operates: A needy family is identified, perhaps staying at a homeless shelter, occupying a rundown house or apartment, or living on the streets. The family's life circumstance is reviewed, and if selected for the program, a project is embarked upon in partnership with them that includes education, job training and placement, and life management instruction. And, of course, a house is built. This structure is erected through a community effort of donated land, materials and labor. The homeless family is involved in the construction, contributing hundreds of hours of labor. This ensures a dignified exchange rather than a handout.

When the project is complete, the family moves into a brand-new house of their own. Their payments are low—interest free—and go into a revolving fund set up by Habitat for Humanity to help future projects. Dignity and ownership are pillars of this approach.

Our suggestion to church leaders: Put to use the wealth of resources in your congregation. Church members may be affiliated with architecture and construction firms, lumber companies, welfare agencies and other helpful resources. You can ensure that your city provides at least one new home a year to the community, a home that becomes the personal property of a needy "resident." If your church is too small to accomplish this alone, involve a consortium of churches in the region. If you are near a university, tap into the energy of Christian college groups; they are always looking for a challenge and outlet for their enthusiasm. Contact Habitat for Humanity for the details on how to proceed (see the resource section). They will provide you with all the information and technical assistance you will need to get started.

A project like this benefits your church as well. Members become motivated to serve in a tangible and practical way; a spirit of unity is engendered by everyone involved; enthusiasm grows as people rally around a common goal; neighbors and the community at large will see that Christians are working to make the world a better place.

10. Feed the Hungry

World Vision, a relief and development ministry, coined an idea in the '70s: How do you feed a hungry world? One person at a time. This notion was in response to the overwhelming sense that there are just too many hungry people and very little that any one person can do about it.

The genius of their approach was to lift us from a feeling of paralysis and give us a manageable response to world hunger. Many of us began to sponsor children; our refrigerators display the photos of kids we support each month. Another great idea was giving sponsors photos of the children they supported. We cannot argue with the innocence of a starving child. We are forced to set aside any subtle prejudicial thoughts that say to the needy, "Don't be lazy—get a job." We have no room for such a condescending attitude when we look into the eyes of a child every time we open the refrigerator door.

World Vision, and dozens of other agencies that offer similar programs, do more than feed children. They bring a broad approach to the community and seek long-term solutions that involve agriculture, industry, job training, education, sanitation, government support and advocacy. They seek to address the entire circumstance while caring for the immediate problem of hunger. The money we send through these sponsorship programs goes beyond the child's daily ration of food.

We view these organizations as a gift from God to the Church. They help us respond to the hungry world in a fashion we could not do by ourselves. And it is a good model of the Body of Christ at work. Here is what we suggest your church do to feed a hungry world:

- Link up with a relief organization in a formal way. Establish a mutual agreement where your church supports their efforts and they provide for you ongoing information and resources about the hungry world. Most of these ministries will provide literature, videos, speakers and programs to involve the youth.

- Contact the Christian Community Development Association (CCDA) for help with reaching the needy in your community. This organization is a collection of ministries that serves inner cities and rural regions of America. They have thought through the various elements that make up wholesome care of the poor, and they provide resources and host an annual conference for those who want to learn more.

- Join the efforts of your local action groups, citizen efforts and city missions to feed the hungry. Many of these groups look for a regular contribution of time and food from local clubs. It would be a great testimony for churches to link up with these groups to show their concern for the hungry. And offer your help all year-round—not just on the traditional Thanksgiving and Christmas "feed days."

11. Problem Solve

People who have run into hard times often need a helping hand to get them back on their feet. People may lack creative ideas and normal resources to pull themselves out of the troublesome situation. They do not think clearly and do not take advantage of helps available to them.

This is where churches come in. They have a way of assembling experts—people, who because of their various backgrounds and career skills, know the local services available to others in distress. A Midwest church decided to set up a regular program for community members who were at the end of their proverbial rope. A weekly meeting was established for people to explain their dilemmas and seek the free and creative input of concerned Christians. The panel of experts included a nurse, lawyer, electrician, teacher, pastor and county welfare employee. Needy people told their stories and sought help. Because the church interceded to meet needs, tangible assistance was provided:

- A mother and father were able to transfer their child into a special education program that addressed his particular learning disabilities.

- A couple was able to forestall eviction from their apartment. They had both lost their jobs and were unable to pay the rent. The panel offered to interface with the landlord and convinced him to be patient while the job search was on. The church members knew that once an unemployed family becomes homeless, they usually have a tough time digging themselves out of the hole. It took a couple of months, but the couple found jobs and stayed in their apartment.

- A single mother was being forced to choose between her job and caring for her new baby. The hours did not fit any affordable child-care options. Rather than watching this woman become another "single-mom statistic," church members got the word out to other single parents. Soon a cooperative was established on the church premises for moms and dads in similar circumstances. Baby-sitting hours were

traded among the parents, services were
exchanged, job networking developed and
a supportive environment was created for
all who participated.

In addition to the practical resources and knowledge
offered to these people in need, the church began to con-
front circumstances that were likely to keep people stuck in
their bad situations. The expert panel encouraged and facil-
itated education, job training, financial management skills
and instruction in proper child care. This proactive approach
is both sensible and compassionate, and this church began
to feel much more connected to its community.

We suggest that this church's model is simple enough
for any other church to follow. Promoting the service was
no problem—word got out fast enough that people flocked
to the church for help.

12. Hold a 'Hands Across...' Event

In 1986, millions of Americans joined hands at the same
moment and stretched in a nearly unbroken line all the
way from the West Coast to the East Coast. People who
held hands paid a small fee to be a part of the event, and
the millions of dollars collected went into a foundation to
feed the hungry. The idea captivated the nation with the
idea of working together for a better world.

We suggest that church leaders get together for a replay
of this idea as an annual event in the local setting. Many
noble secular efforts are constantly in need of more funds.
Imagine the impact of an annual church-sponsored fund-
raiser in which all of the proceeds were given to local service groups. The idea of it alone (money aside) would claim
the attention of those outside the family of faith. Here is
how it might work:

- Link up with as many local pastors as you can. Create a committee that is composed of these church leaders.

- Identify together which local projects you want to help with your effort. Ask these groups to make a presentation to your committee.

- Check the local community calendar for the best date. Let the mayor and chief of police know that a dozen or more churches have joined forces to raise money for civic efforts.

- Allow plenty of lead time to recruit as many church members as possible. The event should include some kind of symbolic linking of hands and then a march to a meeting hall, park or arena for a celebration and handing over of the pledges taken in.

- Of course, let the media know in enough time to cover the event. They are likely to give such an event good coverage. They won't be able to discern any selfish motive—it is a cooperative event and all the funds benefit groups not affiliated with the sponsoring churches.

This sort of effort has the potential of growing into a large annual event. As local citizens hear about the success and integrity of the idea, they may ask to be a part of the event. The church will have taken the leadership in caring for local needs, it will have modeled unity, and it will have demonstrated true compassion for the poor. Not a bad package for a simple notion.

13. Go to the Poor

We believe you should live among the poor for several reasons: first to learn, second to give. It is dangerous to approach the poor with the orientation that you are going to "fix their problems." At no time should we lose the equal footing we all enjoy at the base of the Cross. When going to the poor, we are acknowledging our need to stay sensitive to people who do not have the same material bounty we do. This is a vulnerable deed, because we are staying malleable before the Lord, willing to adjust our lives as prompted. We go to the poor with the genuine desire to make a difference.

Link up with people who work with the poor full time. This will ensure a much more genuine encounter and meaningful contribution. Here are some of the ways we have seen churches go to the poor:

- A church in Washington state sends its entire youth group to Mexico every three years. These young people spend several weeks working on a construction project at an orphanage. The funds for the trip are raised through local community service projects. A relationship has grown over the last 18 years with the same orphanage that serves as the base for the trip. Youth do hard physical labor at the direction of the Mexican staff. You can imagine the long-term impact this has had upon the youth program.

- A Los Angeles church sponsors an annual plunge into several urban ministries in the region. This weeklong trip for high school students is a fast-paced exposure event that

leaves the young people acquainted both with
human need and ministries that are making a
difference in those circumstances. The trip
is wrapped up with debriefing sessions
on what kinds of things these
youth could do long term to help
the poor.

- Several congregations are working with
  churches of other cultures for an
  exchange of resources. Cooperative
  projects are implemented that include
  evangelism, discipleship, agriculture and
  construction. The gifts flow in both
  directions, creating a relationship that
  affirms the dignity of all involved. An organization called Harvest has helped hundreds
  of churches make this link. Their address
  is listed in the resource section.

- More and more churches are sponsoring
  trips for adults, as thousands of men and
  women are using their vacation time to help
  in underserved areas. A service group called
  BridgeBuilders can help you design such a trip.

- Some churches are being a little more
  radical. They are looking at their growing congregations and the need for more space.
  When it is time to move, they do not accept
  the notion that "bigger in the suburbs" is the
  best option for their future. Some actually sell
  their suburban properties and relocate to less
  expensive places in the inner city, where they
  can be more closely aligned with the needy.

14. Give to the Poor

Listed below are six organizations that we believe are well worth your stewardship. They are committed to evangelism and are clear-minded on a wholesome strategy to work with the poor. If you let them know that your church is thinking of becoming involved financially, they will go out of their way to orient you to their programs.

BREAD FOR THE WORLD
802 Rhode Island Ave. NE
Washington, DC 20018
This group is the nation's largest
Christian citizens' lobbying group.
It tries to steer the federal
government toward public
policies that are good for the poor.

BEYOND BORDERS
P.O. Box 7238
St. Davids, PA 19087
This innovative group is a small
Haiti-based ministry that works with
the poor. They work in true partnership
between North Americans and Haitians.

HARAMBEE FAMILY CHRISTIAN CENTER
P.O. Box 40125
Pasadena, CA 91104
This ministry is working to reach the
inner city. Its staff all live among the
people they serve.

WORLD CONCERN
19303 Fremont Ave. North
Seattle, WA 98133
World Concern is a relief and development

organization operated by Christians in
Seattle, Washington.

World Relief
P.O. Box WRC
Wheaton, IL 60189
This is the relief and development arm of
the National Association of Evangelicals.

World Vision
919 W. Huntington Dr.
Monrovia, CA 91016
World Vision is the world's largest
Christian-based relief and development
organization.

15. Spread the Vision for Helping the Poor

Select a day on your annual church calendar to spread the
vision of caring for the poor. Here are some of the ways
you can celebrate that day:

- Organize the church service around God's
  heart for the hungry world. Tell the story of
  Joseph, who was uniquely prepared by God
  to feed the hungry.

- Ask all Sunday School teachers to include
  the theme of serving the poor into their
  lesson that day.

- Create a bulletin insert that gives a brief
  overview of global poverty. Include a
  few "here-is-what-you-can-do-this-week"
  items to provide practical ways to make
  a difference. Remember, it serves no

purpose to overwhelm people with the immensity of the need.

- Ask one of the organizations you sponsor to give a special presentation during the worship service.

- If you have implemented something like the "LoveLoaf" program (through World Vision) to collect money, this would be a good Sunday to break open the loaves.

- Organize a "Saturday Shut-in" for the youth group in conjunction with the special day. No food—just juice and sleeping bags. Show movies to the youth about world hunger and talk about our response. Wrap it up with a pancake feed before the Sunday service.

- Offer a Saturday or Sunday afternoon seminar for those who would like to learn more about world poverty.

16. Resources for Assisting the Poor

Listed below are key Christian resources for you to use as you lead your church in caring for the poor. Also, we encourage you to read the secular publications in your library to stay current with the needs in this country and around the world.

ORGANIZATIONS

BridgeBuilders
9925 Seventh Way N. #102
St. Petersburg, FL 33702
This group will help you set up

a cross-cultural trip for your church members. They specialize in custom-made trips to suit your particular emphasis.

CHRISTIAN COMMUNITY DEVELOPMENT ASSOCIATION (CCDA)

3848 W. Ogden Ave.
Chicago, IL 60623
This organization will help you care for the poor in your own community. In addition to offering many resources, they hold an annual conference and can link you with a ministry in your region.

HABITAT FOR HUMANITY

Habitat and Church Streets
Americus, GA 31709
Habitat for Humanity, well-known because of former President Jimmy Carter's association, is committed to eradicating poverty housing throughout the world.

HARVEST

1979 E. Broadway #2
Tempe, AZ 85282
This group will help you establish a partnership with churches in other cultures.

BOOKS

Fifty Ways You Can Feed a Hungry World by Tony Campolo and Gordon Aeschliman (InterVarsity, 1992).
Rich Christians in an Age of Hunger by Ron Sider (Word, 1990).

State of the Hungry World, an annual published by Bread for the World, Washington, D.C. Bread also puts out an excellent monthly newsletter on world hunger.
Target Earth by Frank Kaleb Jansen (Global Mapping Project, 1989).

CURRICULUM

Cups of Cold Water: Caring for People in Need by Jan Johnson (David C. Cook, 1992).
The Global Issues Bible Study Series edited by Steve Hayner and Gordon Aeschliman (InterVarsity, 1990).

III.
YOUTH
Bridging the Cultural Gap

Jesus had many things to say about young people: "I tell you the truth, unless you change and become like little children, you will never enter the kingdom of heaven" (Matt. 18:3).

"Whoever welcomes one of these little children in my name welcomes me" (Mark 9:37).

"Let the little children come to me, and do not hinder them, for the kingdom of God belongs to such as these" (Luke 18:16).

"Don't let anyone look down on you because you are young" (1 Tim. 4:12).

After reading these verses, can there be any questions regarding God's feeling toward young people?

Children are the heart of the human race. They are born in complete innocence, they carry with them no guile or ill intent, they are not tainted with cynicism and they suffer destruction without comprehension.

Children are the measuring stick of society. They call us back to the center of our existence. They expose the deceitful intentions of our adult minds and force us to examine our motives and deeds. When children are abused, they take upon themselves the very essence of evil; when abandoned, they are the indication of a world that has lost its soul.

We have all seen the sickness. All adults with a shred of compassion grieve over the plight of the innocent. This is today's portrait:

- Five hundred million children will go to bed tonight without a roof over their head and without food in their bellies.

- One hundred million have no family. They live on the streets, where by age eight they will have learned that only the fit and fierce survive. Many will be proficient at robbery and murder before other children can write their names.

- Several million are forced into prostitution in their early teens, servicing grown men and women from Bombay to Brazil, from Los Angeles to Laos. A multibillion-dollar industry of child pornography feeds off this sickness.

- Less than half of the world's youth are able to read a book.

- Several million will never use their minds as adults, because by age five they are so malnourished that their brains have been irreparably damaged.

- A similar number will never use their minds as adults because experimentation with drugs has rendered their intellectual capacities useless.

And what about the Church's role among today's youth? More and more, the Church is becoming irrelevant to this emerging generation. A gap exists much larger than the generation gap of the '60s, and unfortunately, the Church has not seen this gap clearly enough. We need to earnestly seek ways to build bridges to them. The youth of today's world will perhaps be the first truly post-Christian generation. And the blame does not rest entirely with them. The Church's attempts to understand them have been woefully inadequate and inept.

The future of our world and the future of the Church is built upon youth. If we are to ensure a healthy future, a concerted effort must go beyond token outreaches and short-term programs. That process must begin with leaders who are truly heartbroken over the plight of today's young people, leaders who sense a high and holy calling to stand in the gap where society and religion have failed.

The apostle James tells us that true religion is measured by the care of orphans and widows (see Jas. 1:27). Much of today's youth culture has been effectively orphaned by the world. It is time for the Church to parent these children and address their pain as if these kids were their own flesh and blood.

17. Cross the Cultural Divide

It is a big jump!

We know of a church that decided to hire a youth pastor to help them understand and reach their youth. This fellow came with a good deal of experience working with children and teens. It did not take long for him to excite this previously apathetic youth group about following Jesus.

This young leader understood how to use music, media and humor to make the gospel relevant to teens, and in a few months the group had doubled in size. More significantly, the kids were involved in caring for people outside their own circle of friends. As this youth pastor used to say, "You cannot let kids think Christianity is all about doctrine. Doctrine will beat them to death. They've got to see that Jesus doesn't ask us to become like our parents in order to be Christians. They have got to meet Jesus in their own society."

This guy did not know that he was speaking in very sophisticated cross-cultural ministry terms. Never mind, he knew what he was doing and it showed.

Everything was going great, except that older church

members (we are not talking too old—late 30s and up) began to question his methods of ministry. They did not like the earring in his ear and the loud music that came from the group's meeting room. Unfortunately, these adults caused enough of a ruckus that the youth pastor was eventually ousted. You see, the older church members lost the larger war against their youth. Hypocrisy cannot be hidden, and these youth saw it. The kids' suspicions were confirmed: Their parents' faith was all about doctrine and upholding tradition.

We have to be willing to look beyond a piece of jewelry in an ear and strange, blaring music if we want to reach our youth. Aren't they worth it? We suggest that church leaders take very strong steps in the direction of understanding today's youth. Here are a few things that will help:

- Listen to their music. Become familiar enough with it that you go beyond the typical caricatures of it. Try to understand the aspirations expressed in the medium.

- Read their magazines. Go to the local library and ask for a sampling of the most popular youth publications. Make regular stops at the magazine rack to keep up with what kids are reading about.

- Watch a few of the "bizarre" late-night shows that are so popular with this generation.

- Read a few key books that will orient you to this age group. *Thirteenth Gen* by Neil Howe and William Strauss (Vintage Books, 1993) would be a good place to start.

- Understand that today's young people usually are not impressed by the programs we offer.

Institutions and structures are of little value to
them. They place a high value on relationships.

Adult church members will have to give up their prejudices and preconceived ideas if they are going to reach this
generation. They must be willing to experiment, to incorporate new ways of self-expression, to tolerate what they
consider odd behavior. And they must be slow to judge.

Reaching today's youth may seem like a cross-cultural
experience. And any cross-cultural effort is going to involve
elements of the "strange and different." When we do not
understand these new patterns, we may find security in
labeling them as wrong. This kind of judgment will only
widen the gulf between the Church and the youth.

18. Take Your Youth to a Different Culture

A plunge into another culture can be a tremendous way to
become freed from the constraints of our own society.
Sometimes youth reject the Church simply because they do
not have enough exposure to other expressions of faith
and styles of ministry. Our rituals can be too confining, a
prison for those who want try new things. So they may
come to believe that leaving the Church altogether is the
only way to break free of rituals and traditions. We must
encourage teens to develop their own methods of service
and expressions of faith.

We suggest that you organize a variety of cross-cultural
trips for your youth. Here are a few possibilities:

• You may want to start with the very young.
  As mentioned earlier, Youth With a Mission
  (YWAM) has a "Small Half" program that
  involves kids as young as seven and eight
  years old. The program usually lasts for a
  month during the summer and involves Bible

classes, prayer and training in a musical production. Many of these YWAM trips take the kids to perform in other countries.

- Link up with Teen Missions in Florida. They have an excellent program for junior high and high school students. A variety of options are available for a summer of work, excitement and cultural exposure. Some youth will experience five European countries in one summer. The program also includes a basic discipleship component. The first week is shared with 2,000 other youth who have come for the same purpose. The energy of that many young people in one place, all focusing on Jesus, is incredibly challenging and inspirational for those who attend.

- Join forces with Short-Term Evangelical Ministries (STEM), which specializes in youth and college trips that last for one or two weeks. Their expeditions can be tailored to fit your team, and the price is reasonable. All of their programs are conducted in the Caribbean.

- Go to Philadelphia for the summer. Under the auspices of the Evangelical Association for the Promotion of Education (EAPE), you can join 300 other college youth in an inner-city, cross-cultural evangelism and discipleship program. (The address is listed in the resource section).

- Design your own trip. Ask your denomination for contacts in other countries or in nearby inner-city areas. Combine a healthy dose of fun and work. We know one church that wraps up its annual Mexico trip with a two-day blowout at Disneyland.

19. Reach Out to Youth at Risk

Too many of the kids in our communities just do not seem to have much hope. They have already developed drug habits, they skip school regularly, they are sexually active, and they have little connection to the Church.

Reaching them is no small challenge. It is clear that society recognizes these problems. Just look at the number of programs that are targeted at youth: Big Brothers-Big Sisters, YMCA, YWCA, Boy Scouts, Girl Scouts, Pioneer Girls, Boys Brigade, AWANA, Boys and Girls Club, and National Youth Sports, to name a few. Obviously, programs are no substitute for the tender, patient, sincere love of parents toward their own children. But unfortunately, society is not so kind—families do not necessarily come in neat packages anymore. So programs and clubs can at least supplement the instruction and encouragement that many do not get at home.

Here are several ideas on how churches can reach out to children at risk. As a starting point, we suggest that your church leaders forge a partnership with leaders from other congregations. It may be possible to create a local action committee of pastors, lay leaders and parents who feel this is God's calling upon their lives. The efforts could be bathed in persistent prayer and marked by the unified spirit of several groups working together:

- Join efforts with programs that are already in place; no sense in reinventing the wheel. If your town currently has solid youth programs, participate in them and support them. Not only does this avoid needless duplication, but it is also good stewardship of resources and provides the opportunity to build bridges with like-minded people who may not be a part of the faith. It is good for them to see that Christians have the same concerns and desire to help.

- Link up with the local Drug Abuse Resistance Education (DARE) program. In communities across America, this program makes kids aware of drug abuse in the same way the environmental groups instill in kids a deep respect for nature. If your town does not have this program, find out what it would take for your church to implement one.

- Help kids who struggle in school. Meet with local school administrators and teachers to learn why some youth are not keeping up with the curriculum. Ask about the best ways to help these kids overcome their difficulties; for instance, providing volunteer tutors from your congregation or starting an after-school math or reading club. Because some parents might be hesitant to send their child to a church, find a neutral location where this can be offered.

- Survey your local neighborhood to see if there is a need for a latchkey program. Millions of kids go home each afternoon to a house without parents or any form of supervision. Economic realities force some hard choices; parents would be home with their kids if they could, but they must work to earn a living. Most parents would be absolutely thrilled if a local church offered a free after-school program for children until mom or dad came home. Such a program would not only build friends among the community, but it would help prevent kids from getting involved in destructive behaviors.

- Start a sports program. Some churches have found that such programs attract a lot of young people. It does not take a lot of equipment or coordination—a basketball and a hoop will do fine. Have a college student or adult from your congregation be on hand to supervise, coach or referee. A survey of your local area could help discover a surprising number of budding athletes looking for good physical competition.

20. Host a Youth Leaders' Seminar

One way to get the help you need is to ship an expert into your area. Bring in a well-known youth leader for a one-day or weekend seminar to train youth workers from churches in your community. A gathering like this offers several benefits: you will equip your own youth workers; you will bring together local leaders who can trade ideas and offer support; you will set the groundwork for future networking with area churches; and you might talk the expert into hanging around for an extra day to consult your youth staff specifically.

Begin by identifying those local leaders who want to be part of a group effort. Pray together that the Lord will turn you into a real team of coworkers. Coordinate the church calendars and determine the best possible date. Then contact potential speakers for the event (Youth Specialties or the National Institute of Youth Ministry are great resources). Tell them you have a group of youth leaders from several churches who are gathering for a weekend, and negotiate a rate that is within everyone's budget. Create a flyer for other pastoral staff and lay leaders in the area, and recruit heavily for the event. Youth Specialities usually offers a package that runs from Friday evening to late Saturday afternoon.

You may want to connect an evening youth concert to the event. Use the network of pastors who come to the seminar to promote the Saturday night concert. This idea has a couple of benefits. The most obvious is providing good entertainment for your youth. You will also create an event on the heels of your seminar, an event that is contemporary and reminds you of the cultural wall you are attempting to scale. The concert could serve as a tangible encouragement to the youth workers who attend the seminar—something can be done cooperatively.

Some of the leaders may want to extend the experience into future years. Youth Specialties hosts the nation's premier annual National Youth Workers Convention. Their seminar roster is unmatched. At least a thousand youth leaders consider this their annual refueling station.

21. Go to the Street Kids

We have already suggested ways to get your youth across cultures to influence their walk with Christ. It would be valuable for the church's youth leaders and other key adults to travel to some parts of the world where the plight of youth is particularly stark. We believe these trips are good stewardship. They permanently imprint on our minds the images of the "least of these" and forever alter our behavior and leadership.

Consider including both national and international excursions. For a good East Coast exposure to youth at risk, contact Kingdom Works in Philadelphia. They could customize a tour for you. On the West Coast, contact World Impact for a close-up on Los Angeles (both addresses in the resource section).

For an international trip, we suggest you contact a couple of options: Action International Ministries, based in the Seattle area, has a strong ministry in the Philippines and Brazil, specifically with street kids. They have pioneered the work of Two-Thirds World street kids. For exposure to Western youth at risk, check out YWAM Amsterdam. They have a staff of 300 young adults working in the center of Amsterdam's red-light district. Their work not only touches the lives of thousands of young adults who face a bleak future, but their work also trains hundreds of Christians each year in the ministry of reaching urban youth.

22. Give to the Youth

How do children first learn stewardship at church? Heavy sermons on tithing? Hearing the message "you ought to or else"? Graphs showing progress on the fund drive for a building project? Of course not.

We think it makes sense to teach stewardship in a context that makes giving real and tangible for children. And what could be more real than seeing little kids who live on the streets at night, do not have parents and do not have enough food to eat? It is important to give our children the opportunity to share their own wealth and to find meaningful channels for their stewardship.

Here is what we suggest: Bring your youth leaders and Sunday School teachers together to discuss the idea. Lead a brainstorming session to bring out all the creative ways youth could be encouraged to give. Think through the different kinds of street ministries that might capture the imagination of your young people. Obviously, you will need to find a variety of ideas to tie in with the different age groups. Think of something both local and abroad. It would be great if they could get some kind of hands-on experience to make the need more meaningful to them.

Perhaps some age levels could create posters that illustrate the plight of street kids. Old magazines are great resources for this. A special "kids room" could be designed in the church as a place to carry all sorts of visual reminders of global needs. A large bulletin board could carry clips from newspaper articles or current publications. Youth could be encouraged to keep the board updated. Don't miss the chance to involve the first and second graders in this. They are particularly open to learning, and they have a natural compassion for people in need.

Each class level could set its own donation goal. They could choose where to send their money and how much. Several youth groups already do this; they take on local work projects to help meet their giving goal. And then once a month or once a year, the funds are mailed off with appropriate pomp and fanfare.

This way, children learn that financial stewardship is not a lofty concept for projects they cannot understand or visualize. Giving becomes more than plunking a few quarters in the offering plate. A hands-on plan makes the experience real. In time they will find it natural to graduate to giving that is more complex and demanding.

23. Spread the Vision for Youth

Put an annual Youth Day on the church calendar. Here are some of the items that could be incorporated:

- Have the sermon and Sunday School lessons focus on children. You can take plenty of approaches from the Scriptures—stories of how God worked through children, Jesus' teaching about young ones, examples of children's faith.

- Involve young people in the service. Perhaps some could report on ministry trips or outreach experiences. Those talented in music or drama could perform. You might even let a promising youth give a 10-minute sermon from the pulpit.

- If you implemented a special youth stewardship plan, this Sunday would be a good time to report on where the money is going and to pray for those various ministries. Ask a representative from each age group to lead the church in prayer for the ministry they have been supporting.

- Create a bulletin insert that describes the plight of youth around the world. Include practical "what-you-can-do-about-it" tips.

- Offer a special youth seminar on Saturday or Sunday afternoon for those who want to explore the subject further. That could be the time to sponsor the Youth Leaders' Seminar we mentioned earlier and to offer an evening youth concert.

24. Resources for Reaching Youth

We have found the following resources to be a tremendous help in working with youth:

ORGANIZATIONS

Action International Ministries (AIM)
P.O. Box 490
Bothell, WA 98014
Contact AIM for help with designing an outreach to street kids in the Philippines and Brazil.

THE EVANGELICAL ASSOCIATION FOR THE PROMOTION OF EDUCATION (EAPE)
P.O. Box 238
St. Davids, PA 19087
This is Tony Campolo's
ministry to inner-city youth.

KINGDOM WORKS
10 Lancaster Ave.
Wynnewood, PA 19096
This group will help you
gain greater exposure
to youth in the
Philadelphia region.

NATIONAL INSTITUTE OF YOUTH MINISTRY
940 Calle Amanecer, Suite G
San Clemente, CA 92672
This group trains and equips
youth workers internationally.

SHORT-TERM EVANGELICAL MINISTRIES (STEM)
P.O. Box 290066
Minneapolis, MN 55429
This group will help you put
together a trip to the Caribbean.

TEEN MISSIONS
885 East Hall Road
Merritt Island, FL 32953
Teen Missions sponsors high
school students in cross-cultural
ministry opportunities in order
to give an understanding
of God's call to missions.

World Impact

2001 S. Vermont Ave.
Los Angeles, CA 90007
This group can give you a
tour of the Los Angeles area.

Young Life

P.O. Box 520
Colorado Springs, CO 80901
This ministry will often capture
the imagination of youth where
the church was unable to make
a connection. They offer clubs in
every state.

Youth With a Mission (YWAM)

Prince Hendrikkade 50, 1012
AC Amsterdam, The Netherlands
Contact them for information
about ministry opportunities in
Amsterdam.

Youth Specialties

1224 Greenfield Dr.
El Cajon, CA 92021
Youth Specialties is the premier
source for advice on youth
ministry. They are contemporary,
practical and experienced.
Inquire about their national
youth conference and the
award-winning *Youthworker Journal.*
This journal is the nation's
leading publication for ministry
to youth.

BOOKS

*The Complete Student Mission
Handbook* by Noel Becchetti
(Youth Specialties, 1990).
Youth and Missions by
Paul Borthwick (Victor, 1988).

MAGAZINES

Campus Life Magazine, Carol Stream, IL.
Youthworker Journal (described on
previous page).

IV.
MISSIONS
Reaching a World in Need

God is always pursuing the world with His love. This is not a doctrinal concept—it is personal. Since the beginning of time, God has desired relationship with the crown of creation. The story of Adam and Eve shows us a God who walked through the garden for a personal chat with loved ones (see Gen. 2 and 3). The Old Testament is filled with stories of a King who pleads with His followers to remain linked to Him: If you put away your heart of stone, I will be your God and you will be my people. "My people" is one of the common phrases of the Old Testament.

God was never satisfied to constrain His love to the people of Israel. When Abraham begins his first journey of faith to a place God would yet show him, Yahweh announces, "I will make your name great, and you will be a blessing....and all peoples on earth will be blessed through you" (Gen. 12:2,3). This theme of "all peoples" is a golden thread that winds itself through the Law, the Psalms and the Prophets. The Israelites understood that their Lord wanted to raise every valley and lower every mountain to make straight the path that led to the mountain of Zion. The very Temple was designed with a courtyard that was meant to hold the scores of foreigners who would come to worship Yahweh.

Israel was selfish in its call to spread the good news of Yahweh. Indeed, when Christ is headed toward the crucifixion, He clears the Temple with the judgment, "My house will be called a house of prayer for all nations? But you have made it a 'den of robbers'" (Mark 11:17). The very area intended for all nations to worship had been turned into a money-making plaza. Jesus continues resolutely toward the cross and as He gives up His breath, the curtain that barred the public from the holy of holies is ripped in two—top to bottom. The message seems to be, "Never again shall a people prevent others from enjoying My salvation." Christ's body, broken for the world. The disciples caught on to the notion. Historians tell us that 11 of them died as martyrs on the mission field, Thomas as far away as North India.

The book of Revelation promises us a good ending to the effort of Calvary—one day members from every tribe, tongue and nation will celebrate the complete and final work of the Cross (see Rev. 7:9,10).

Missions, at its core, is nothing more than the Church living out the global nature of God's love. God wills that none should perish. We, His Church are filled with the same heart and work to establish His love in all the earth. The truth is, all of us are the product of "foreign missions." The Church began as a small Jewish movement in Palestine. Over the centuries, this band of believers expanded their reach to all corners of the earth, and now it is fair to say that the sun never sets on the Church of Jesus Christ.

But the mission to reach the world is far from over. Perhaps as many as two billion people still live outside the family of faith. And as many as half of them do not know the name of Jesus to mean anything in particular. The good news has not become a meaningful option to them.

The missionary movement is very much alive. More than 250,000 Christians live full time in another culture expressly for the purpose of telling people about Jesus. These people are not all white. They represent the full mosaic of God's creation—red, brown, yellow, black and white—and they hail from every country in the world. They are noble servants of love. Their sacrifice is pleasing to God, and their lives are an inspiration to Christians the world over.

Of course, the style of missions has changed. What once seemed a fairly consistent image—pith helmet, bushwhacker, khaki pants—is an outdated portrait that has no relevance today. Because of the lack of technology and resources, those missionaries faced incredible hardship. And when their ships pushed away from shore, the likelihood that they would ever see home again was slim. By contrast, the missionary of today flies frequently between continents, phones home to wish friends a happy birthday and may also pack a computer for transcontinental communication.

We need to adjust our perception of the missionary and our understanding of mission work. But we must not let go of this calling. As long as we accept the responsibility to lead the church, we also must accept the challenge to lead in the global mission of the Church.

25. Encourage Working Abroad

The old term for it was "tentmaking." Simply put, it is the idea that your missionary work is funded by your job.

Today, more than 400,000 North American Christians live abroad and are employed by a secular company. Their responsibilities are as diverse as teaching, administrating hospitals, promoting government programs, designing sewer systems and managing telecommunications systems. These people enjoy the benefits of a regular salary, medical coverage, vacation and extended leave options back home—often paid for by their employer.

This is welcome news for those who have some sense of a cross-cultural calling. The post-World War II model of missions is too cumbersome for many people who are gifted at serving God overseas but not skilled at fund-raising. A typical missionary family today is expected to raise upward of $60,000 a year. Very few of us could even begin to think of such a challenge as manageable. Hundreds of eager missionary-families-in-waiting give up after a couple of years of going from church to church in search of funds without raising an adequate amount.

The tentmaking option is not a "cop-out" for people who could not—or did not want to—raise support. It is a marvelous gift from God that makes the likelihood of missionary service real for thousands more people than would have been possible just decades ago. We have to adjust our traditional views if we are to take advantage of the contemporary opportunities. Here is what we suggest:

- Talk to your church members about the idea of taking a job abroad. Share with them the vision of ministering overseas while working for a company that will foot the bill. Challenge members to consider one- or two-year work options that take them to another culture. If some show interest, pray together regularly and begin to plot a course of action.

- Get help from tentmaking organizations (we have listed a first-rate one, USAT, in the resource section). These groups will help minimize frustrations and maximize ministry opportunities. Some keep an up-to-date listing of international job openings.

- When church members go to serve as tentmakers, send them off with the full support and honor you would confer on traditional missionaries. Commit to pray regularly for them and, if possible, visit them while abroad. If you have a listing of full-time missionaries who are supported by the church, be sure these tentmakers are included.

26. Host Internationals

Several million internationals are in the United States on temporary visas. Fourteen percent of them are Muslim. More than 300,000 are university students from China.

Most of these people are leaders (or future leaders) back home—in industry, education or government. The missionary movement would not have dreamed of this opportunity just a generation ago. Although we do not support the notion of "head-hunting" for the Lord, we do believe that if God brings people outside the faith into contact with us, we at least want to build a friendship and pray for them. God may intend our lives to be a bridge toward redemption.

We also think that contact with internationals can help to break down prejudices we so often carry regarding other cultures. In the United States, we have been subtly taught to accept a racist and unflattering view of Muslims. The Church has often propagated this view during times of conflict between Israel and neighboring Arab countries. Our tendency is to generalize that all Arabs are like Moammar Qaddafi and Saddam Hussein. We need contact with internationals so that our minds can be redeemed of these stereotypes.

Here are a few suggestions for hosting internationals:

- Sponsor cultural evenings at the church. Invite internationals who have become friends to share a special food, music, art or dress. Perhaps they could do a presentation on literature, history or their country's dominant religion. This exchange affirms the dignity of all involved while teaching us more about another culture.

- Volunteer to help internationals adjust to this culture. Universities in particular are looking for people to assist foreign students with language, currency, transportation systems, the grocery store and local ordinances that could affect them.

- Offer to have internationals live in your home. Many are looking for a good break on room and board and would love to get closer to the American culture through a live-in arrangement. You can place ads in local school newspapers or submit your name to the university housing office.

- Invite internationals to attend traditional celebrations, such as Thanksgiving and Christmas. Structure these get-togethers specifically for the guests, and explain that the evening is designed as an introduction to American culture.

27. Focus on Unreached Peoples

If there is such a thing as the "final frontier of missions," it is those areas outside the shadow of the Church. As we mentioned before, as many as one billion people have no idea what or who Jesus is. The single largest group of such people are the Muslims. There are almost a billion Muslims in the world today, and many of them have great respect for Jesus because the Koran elevates Him. Others, though, have learned hand-me-down versions of this "prophet" who is supposedly the product of Allah and a woman. The notion is so reprehensible that Christianity is simply not an option to them.

Missionary work to the unreached peoples of the world is perhaps the closest we can get to the older model of missions. This work often requires building relationships with people who live in closed societies. They are suspicious of foreigners, they do not employ modern technology, and they are tightly knit in a web of relationships that equates conversion with a rejection of family. This is a notion very unfamiliar to our society.

Gearing up members in your church to become involved in missions to unreached peoples is no small task. The commitment requires immense preparation, study and training. It is long-term, which cuts against our cultural norm that stresses mobility and shallow roots. Our suggestion is that you bring in experts to highlight the exciting and rich opportunities of working among unreached peoples. Several organizations and seminar leaders will be happy to help. Here are a few (their addresses are listed in the resource section):

- The Zwemer Institute is the nation's leading center for orienting Christians to the work with Muslims. Their staff can host a "Muslim Awareness Seminar" at your church or simply share information with your church leaders. Their seminars are especially good at teaching people to appreciate the immense contributions Arabs have made to Western society.

- "Destination 2000" is a seminar designed by Bob Sjogren of Frontiers, another ministry to unreached peoples. The seminar is a weekend package that lays out the biblical call to minister to all peoples. The seminar can be presented in person or on video.

- "Perspectives on the World Christian Movement" is a college-level course taught in 50 different locations in the United States. It is set up as a class: 20 lectures spread over 10 weeks, including reading assignments and

tests. (A class typically meets for 10
Monday nights in a row, each evening
lasting 3½ hours.) College credit is
available for those who take this seminar.
Often, several churches will cosponsor the
course. Coordinators are asked to go
through a training course before
offering the class.

28. Join the Short-term Mission Party

This is the fastest-growing phenomenon in mission work
today. As many as 250,000 local church members take part
in short, cross-cultural mission trips each year. There is good
reason for this, of course. In our day of rapid transportation
and modern technology, it makes sense to explore. God
has gifted us with curious minds; it is natural to learn. More
than that, God has put within us a love for the world.

A benefit of short-term projects that is not always adver-
tised is its value to the congregation. Many pastors are
deeply committed to these cross-cultural excursions for no
other reason than they light a fire inside their church members. A pastor-friend of ours says it is *the* key to his discipleship program and that it would be the church's last budget item to go.

One large church created the notion of a "Vacation With
a Purpose" (VWAP). Their brilliant idea was to help church
members have more meaningful vacations. The trips, planned
by the church, all target Central America and the Caribbean
to keep costs down. The idea was a great success, and now
other churches are following suit. A book and leader's guide
on VWAP have been published by NavPress.

If you are interested in organizing a short-term project for your church, here are two organizations that can
help (others are listed in the resource section):

- BridgeBuilders is a "one-stop" resource for your short-term mission needs. They will custom-make a trip specifically for your church. They can offer the full range of services, from booking your tickets to designing the program, from teaching the devotionals to coordinating the construction effort. They listen carefully to what you want and then create the package around that request.

- The second group, Discover the World, is aimed more specifically at leaders. They will send a team into your church and train you how to run your own program. And although they do not broker specific experiences for you, they will train your team and provide Bible study materials to take abroad.

29. Study Abroad

Pastors and other church leaders should plan to continually broaden their understanding of the world. It is not unreasonable to spend two weeks of every year in an entirely new location. Pastors are given the responsibility to lead their churches into all the world. It makes good sense to stay sharp in global affairs. An annual trip will also keep the commitment to reaching the world sharp. When we regularly brush against the pain of the world, we cannot intellectualize it or shrug it off. We have to ask, "Lord, what will you have me do?"

Most churches offer a regular study benefit to their pastors. Some denominations require it of all their pastors. The idea is good: Leaders have to keep learning if they are to continue leading.

In planning your annual trip, we recommend the following guidelines:

- Go for variety. If you were in Brazil last year, go to Japan this year and Kenya next year. If you were visiting the slums last year, stay in a high-rise this year and a rural area next year. Try for exposure to various forms of government and dominant religions.

- Occasionally build in a language school. Several two-week options are available to gain intensive exposure to Spanish, French and German, to name a few. Language is a key that lets you into different cultures.

- Plan some trips to theological institutions. The broad array of Third World and European seminaries can make for an invaluable lesson in culture. We do not often see how closely our theological views reflect our cultural fabric. Exposure to another culture's theological tenets can open up concepts or portions of Scripture that earlier were a mystery or irrelevant.

30. Give to Missions

There is no doubt that sending out Western missionaries is expensive. Some people argue that it is poor stewardship to support missionaries when nationals can do the same job for much less money. If we looked only at the economic grid, that would be true. For example, the salary package of one United States missionary family in India could support 30 Indian missionary families doing the identical work. But we cannot always look at economics. The mystery of the Body must always be upheld in our Church life. We must model unity in a world that is ravaged by division. Furthermore, we all contribute unique gifts to God's work. For that reason, we must continue to support Western missionaries, even if the bill seems extreme.

Having said that, there is very little direct support to nationals who are doing the work of missions. Most funds going to these people are handled by agencies that siphon off questionable chunks for overhead. We have listed three groups below that we think are doing a unique work and could benefit from the gracious giving of the North American church. Write to them for more information on how you can partner with them in ministry.

We know your funds will be used with utmost integrity and will go far in touching people's lives. If you are attached to a denomination, contact the main office for ways to connect with national ministries. Your church could link up with them directly and over time enjoy a fruitful relationship of mutual exchange.

Gospel for Asia
1932 Walnut Plaza
Carrollton, TX 75006
This ministry, operated by
an Indian, has more than
3,000 full-time missionaries.

Youth Alive Ministries
P.O. Box 129
Orlando 1804
Soweto
Republic of South Africa
This ministry has a key impact on the
future black youth of South Africa. The
organization is operated entirely by

blacks and the headquarters
are centered where the need
is the greatest.

YOUTH FOR CHRIST
P.O. Box 1311
Colombo
Sri Lanka
The nation of Sri Lanka is terribly
divided along religious lines. Thousands of
people have died over the last decade due
to religious violence. It is particularly tough
to be a Christian there, and most expatri-
ates have fled. This branch of Youth for
Christ is operated by nationals.

31. Spread the Vision for Mission Work

Mission conferences are common in evangelical churches.
If you do not currently sponsor one, we suggest you mark
your annual calendar for at least one Sunday a year that
focuses on world missions. Here are some of the things
you could do that day:

- Have the sermon and Sunday School teaching
  center on worldwide missions.

- If any of your church members went on a
  short-term project during the previous year,
  this would be a good time to have them report
  on their experiences. You could also promote
  next year's trips.

- Create a bulletin insert that gives some statistics on world missions. Offer a few pointers on
  what a typical family can do to help.

- Arrange for a missionary to give a presentation on his or her work.

- If any of your members have lived abroad (for school or business), ask them to talk about their experiences.

- Create an international banquet after church. Contact local visiting internationals and ask them to provide their cuisine at your expense.

- Offer a Saturday afternoon seminar on missions for those who would like to know more.

32. Resources for Missions

ORGANIZATIONS

ASSOCIATION OF INTERNATIONAL MISSION SERVICES (AIMS)

P.O. Box 64534
Virginia Beach, VA 23464
This organization specializes in helping Charismatic churches become involved in missions.

ACMC

P.O. Box ACMC
Wheaton, IL 60189
ACMC helps churches to organize missions committees into established programs that will motivate congregations to become more involved in missions.

BRIDGEBUILDERS

9925 Seventh Way N. #102
St. Petersburg, FL 33702
This organization is a full-service short-term

mission broker. They can help you create a short trip that is tailor-made to your needs.

Discover the World
3255 E. Orange Grove Blvd.
Pasadena, CA 91107
This group will train you to design your own short-term mission project.

USAT
500 W. University, Box 61163
Shawnee, OK 74801
USAT finds employment for Christians who want to serve abroad as tentmaking missionaries.

BOOKS
Fifty Ways You Can Reach the World by Tony Campolo and Gordon Aeschliman (InterVarsity, 1993).
How to Be a World-Class Christian by Paul Borthwick (Victor, 1991).
Romancing the Globe: The Call of the Wild on Generation X by Gordon Aeschliman and Dan Harrison (InterVarsity, 1993).
Unleashing a Wild Hope by Tom Sine (Word, 1992).
Vacations With a Purpose by Chris Eaton and Kim Hurst (NavPress, 1991).

HANDBOOKS
MARC Handbook, 15th Edition
919 W. Huntington Dr.
Monrovia, CA 91016
This lists the 700-plus North American agencies involved in missions. Several

helpful charts and articles accompany the statistics and resource information.

Short-Term Mission Handbook
701 Main St.
Evanston, IL 60202
This is the complete industry handbook on short-term missions.

NEWSLETTERS

MARC Newsletter
919 W. Huntington Dr.
Monrovia, CA 91016
This newsletter is written for leaders who want to stay current on resources for international missions.

World Pulse
P.O. Box 794
Wheaton, IL 60189
This publication provides the latest news and trends in missions.

SEMINARS

DESTINATION 2000
P.O. Box 40159
Pasadena, CA 91114

MUSLIM AWARENESS SEMINAR
P.O. Box 365
Altadena, CA 91001

**PERSPECTIVES ON THE
WORLD CHRISTIAN MOVEMENT**
1605 Elizabeth St.
Pasadena, CA 91114

CONFERENCES

MIAMI SHORT-TERM MISSION CONFERENCE
P.O. Box 52-7900
Miami, FL 33152
This is the nation's top annual conference for leaders who want to gain tools to lead short-term teams. It is held the last weekend of January.

URBANA
P.O. Box 7895
Madison, WI 53707
Every three years, between Christmas and New Year's, IVCF convenes the massive student mission convention in Urbana, Illinois. The event draws 20,000 people for five days and sets the North American mission agenda for the next three years.

V.
THE ENVIRONMENT
Tending God's Creation

We truly do worship an awesome God. Sit back for a moment and reflect on the process of creation—not the short narrative we have in Scripture, but rather all the details and complexities that went into those days. There are millions of different flowers in the world. God specifically "penciled" out the shape of each, blended the watercolors and matched the leaves to the petals. He decided which varieties should grow in the various climates, how they should group themselves on the edge of a hill in early spring and how they should lay a carpet across a meadow. Trees and shrubs were added. Hundreds of varieties of grasses were brushed in. Waterfalls, rivers and underground springs were strategically placed to contrast the greens, bubble over rocks and provide sustenance to the delicate plants.

And that is just the beginning. Let your mind wander through the diverse flocks of birds, ducks and geese. Picture the design and placement of jaguars, foxes, raccoons, badgers, elephants and deer. Sink into the deep oceans and imagine the million-plus pieces of art that swim in an underground world of delight that is much like a private aquarium for the Creator.

Design a sunset. A sunrise. Push the ocean's floor up through the billions of tons of water and make an island from molten rock. Dot the sky with stars overhead. Place in orbit the planets with their mystical rings and moons.

All of this is the personal handiwork of the same God who was viciously strung up on a piece of wood.

It is nothing but pure blasphemy and disrespect for us to run rampant over the creative work of God. "This is my Father's world," says the hymn, and so it is. All of this is the Lord's and the fullness thereof. People who love Jesus would no more destroy the environment than they would rip to shreds the carefully painted canvas of a best friend. And yet it is curious how many Christians do not seem to care.

The Church has been silent far too long. We have allowed those outside the faith to define our obligation to care for the "garden." We have, in fact, withdrawn from our duty to tend it. Worse, we often label people who care for the earth as being "liberal" or "New Age."

When we care for the environment, we show our deep respect for the Creator in the same way we would admire the work of a great artist in a museum. Make no mistake, the world sees our treatment of creation and unconsciously picks up the message regarding our disrespect. When we care about God's handiwork, we demonstrate our love for God, and that speaks volumes to the world.

What is more, caring for creation is a way of caring for ourselves. Nature has a way of ministering back to us. It provides color, shapes, scents, shade and sustenance. Tending creation is also showing consideration for our children's future. We love them enough to provide a clean and beautiful garden that paints a stunning picture of the artist.

There is nothing suspicious about loving the environment. But there is something awfully suspicious and wrong about trampling it. Doesn't it make sense that those who personally love the Creator would be the ones to take a personal interest in His handiwork?

Next time you pass a rose, stop and smell it. After all, it's naturally Christian to do so.

33. Green the City

Why not showcase God's artistry in your city? Christians sometimes find it difficult to find common ground with people outside the faith. Well, caring for the earth is a natural and friendly way to come together. There is no "catch" to this one—no literature or speeches that try to convince people to join the Christian faith. Just a wonderful spot of beauty for whoever wants to enjoy it.

There are several ways to green the city. Some ideas are listed below, starting with the most simple to the more complex. Pick the level that suits your situation. You may want to join with several churches in your region to take on the more ambitious projects. Whatever level you choose, approach city hall with a clear offer: You want to help keep the city beautiful—nothing more. You are offering to do the planning, the work and handle the expense.

- Landscape the sidewalks or medians of a specific section of town—perhaps a couple of city blocks. Some communities already have "adopt-a-block" programs. If there is one in your area, join in. If there is not, you be the first.

- Plant trees on city- or county-owned property that is unlikely to be developed. Make it an annual event rather than a one-time offer. You will need to coordinate with city planners to find out the areas available and the types of trees and shrubs they would like planted.

- Landscape a city monument or historical building. City budgets are shrinking all the time, so your local officials would probably be happy to have someone lend a hand. This allows for a lot of creative expression and could lead to some good publicity.

- Create a minipark. Not a large recreational facility, of course, but a walk-and-sit kind of place where you bring your picnic basket for a slow lunch. If the land is designed well, you could include a small pond with ducks and fish.

- Establish a natural reserve. Some leaders are ambitious enough to dream about a 40-acre property that includes a small forest, a couple of ponds, a large greenhouse and a visitor's center complete with hands-on science and wildlife displays for kids. Literature could describe the natural habitat of the region, list ways to be more environmentally friendly at home and suggest additional field trips in the area. Schools could take their students through the reserve, and artists could come to capture the beauty of it. A small store could sell art, crafts and literature that encourage stewardship of the environment.

If you take on one of these larger projects, you may want to look for professionals within your church (or partnering churches) who are knowledgeable in horticulture, landscaping, architecture and planning. Cities have to watch out for liability and labor concerns. You can actually do your work on a contract basis where your nonprofit group is hired to do the job but at donated labor rates (free). You already carry liability insurance for your church programs, so the precedent is well established.

34. Green the Church

Our daily routines at church often are detrimental to the environment. Not that we pour poisons into the air or slash and burn trees, but in small ways we needlessly harm creation. One of the benefits of the environmental movement is that it has taught ordinary folk—not just the experts—that we are all able to make a difference.

Plenty of resources are available to show us the benefits of recycling and reducing waste. If you take leadership to make sure your church's habits are friendly to the environment, you will have instituted patterns that become a daily reminder that we worship the Lord of Creation—and therefore we are taking good care of His "garden."

Below we list several ways you can begin to "green your church" if you have not already done so. Check out the resource section if you want to take this idea further. The book *Fifty Ways You Can Help Save the Planet* is full of specific ideas. The Christian Environmental Association can send you a "Green Your Church" kit (see address in resource section).

- Use overheads instead of handouts. When possible, project announcements or choruses on a screen rather than printing them on a sheet of paper.

- At church functions, be careful to avoid waste. When possible, use plates, cups and silverware that can be washed. Thousands of trees get thrown away each Sunday across America because we use paper plates and cups at coffee hours and after-church suppers. And stamp out Styrofoam. It is almost impossible to recycle.

- Create a system to collect all newspapers, magazines, used office paper and junk mail. These can be recycled. Make it an office policy that trash bins exist only for materials that cannot be recycled. If you follow this diligently, you will rarely empty the trash.

- Have a plumber check all the church fittings. You may be surprised to discover how many thousands of gallons of water you are losing each month because of leaks. Water is a precious resource, and it costs money.

- Ask the local utility company to inspect your energy drain. You will probably be able to conserve significantly with a few minor repairs and changes in behavior.

- Post a few signs around the church to make the case for recycling. Involve the youth group; they have probably been taught this at school. Ask them to design posters that show the link between caring for the environment and our relationship to the Creator.

- Beautify your church grounds. Earlier we encouraged you to consider beautifying the city; you can start at your church. This does not have to be an expensive affair. Identify people in the church who are interested and ask them to help add trees, shrubs and flowers to the grounds.

35. Establish a Recycling Center

Every Sunday, millions of people drive to church. What a natural setup for recycling! The plan is simple: Ask members to bring their recycled goods to church each week. Youth have been well trained to think about the environment, so recruit them to serve as the Green Brigade. As cars drive up, have them gather whatever goods are brought. Have bins available to hold the variety of materials—aluminum, glass, paper and tin. Make the process as easy as possible.

Go a step further if you are able. Advertise your church as a drop-off point for anyone in town. Build bins large enough and make instructions clear enough so anyone can stop by to drop off their goods. Because some community members might be skeptical about where the proceeds will go, consider donating the money to a project everyone can appreciate, such as a Youth at Risk program or college scholarship fund (mention this in your advertisements). This kind of vision would excite city officials and definitely draw some good reviews from the local newspaper.

36. Join the Earth Day Celebration

Every year, April 22nd is Earth Day. Citizens across the nation celebrate it with special clean-up efforts, recycling drives, reforestation projects, parades, speeches and much flag waving. It makes a lot of sense for churches to be right in the middle of these activities.

This could make some people uncomfortable. "You mean mix with those New Agers and Earth-First types? What if someone should see us?" That is the whole idea! For starters, Christians are meant to live in the world (see John 17:15). That concept is part of our very identity because we follow the One who left heaven in order to *live in the world*. And how else do we expect to make friends with New Agers if we do not hang around them?

Working together on an Earth Day project is a natural setting for building relationships. It is not contrived. Your involvement could even be a nice kind of shock for these folk. Many of them would not imagine that Christians care much about creation. Do not worry if it appears you are endorsing strange beliefs by involving yourself with this group. It is God-honoring to care for creation, and that is why you are doing it. Be careful not to turn the cooperative effort into an opportunity to "correct" others' beliefs. Allow the common interest to provide a bridge for long-term friendships.

If your town does not already have some sort of Earth Day celebration, take the lead. Here are a few ideas:

- Work with the local library and school teachers to have children design posters on the subject of caring for the earth. Create categories such as animals, plants and human relationships.

- Sponsor a photography contest for display at a local mall.

- Work with your local newspaper to hold a contest featuring essays on the earth. Create several levels of entry, and have the winning pieces published on Earth Day.

- If you are up for a big challenge, work with other churches, local clubs, civic groups and schools to sponsor an Earth Day parade down Main Street.

37. Take God's Beauty to an Inner-City Area

If your church is located outside of the city, see if you can partner with an inner-city ministry to bring the beauty of creation to their area. Often, these groups must travel to the countryside to see trees and flowers. To them, the inner city remains depressing, drab and ugly. It need not be so. Here are a couple of ways you could work together:

- Offer to do modest landscaping of their grounds. Look for ways to plant trees, shrubs and flowers that bring back a sense of God's beauty. Carry the load of both the finances and the initial work. These ministries are often so overworked that adding something else could be overwhelming. You may discover that young people in the area or associated with the ministry show interest in the project. If so, involve them in planning the next round of planting and teach them the art of maintaining a healthy garden.

• Offer to set up and maintain a small fruit and vegetable garden. In most regions of the United States, it is easy to get a healthy crop of some sort—apples, peaches, strawberries, tomatoes, peppers, lettuce or carrots. The experience of watching the garden grow from a dormant seed to mature fruit is inspirational in itself. But the experience also puts the power of creation right into our hands. That kind of lesson goes far with people who are used to feeling like the victims of creation.

38. Give to the Earth

The Bible tell us that creation groans, barely able to wait for the day of redemption (see Rom. 8:21,22). We believe that is not just a poetic picture but that it is real. Every day, the earth absorbs tons of our poisons, loses vast acreage of covering and breathes in voluminous amounts of toxins belched from our machinery of modern living. And our human behaviors are erasing the last remaining places of untouched earth. At this pace, our grandchildren won't know a rain forest from a garbage dump.

We have an excellent idea for saving the earth: Join a Christian movement that is buying up land to preserve the last outposts of creation. The Christian Environmental Association is a nonprofit ministry that is, among other things, purchasing large portions of tropical moist and rain forests in Central America. They call this their Eden Conservancy program. As properties are purchased, a small station is established so select groups can tour the location to see the beauty God created and to ensure it stays beautiful.

Your church can help buy these Eden lands. For as little as $100, your church can purchase a full acre of rain forest for the Conservancy. Youth easily connect to the value of this idea. Fund-raisers can be established through recycling and can be matched with straight donations by the adults. Each Sunday School class could plan to sponsor its own acre. In time, your church alone could help preserve several hundred acres of tropical land.

We need to be bold and creative with our stewardship notions. In 50 years it will be too late to think about establishing an Eden Conservancy. The acreage will be denuded if present rates of deforestation continue. Today's generation of Christian leaders has the unique opportunity of helping to spare the last of the great forests from destruction.

39. Spread the Vision for the Environment

Make Earth Day a part of your annual church calendar. Get it as close to April 22nd as possible. Here are some of the things you could do as part of that annual celebration:

- Have the sermon and Sunday School
  teaching center around the theme of caring
  for creation.

- Describe the current global situation.
  Suggest simple steps to take care of creation.

- Explain the church's commitment
  to recycling.

- If you want to become involved in the Eden Conservancy program, this would be a great Sunday to collect the funds for it. Perhaps you could break it down by members—100 members giving one dollar each purchases one full acre of rain forest.

- If you want to kick off a recycling program or "green the city" effort, this Sunday would be the perfect time to launch it.

- Offer a Saturday or Sunday afternoon seminar on the environment for those who want to learn more.

- If your town has an Earth Day parade, strongly urge your members to join the event as a clear statement that Christians love the creation of their Lord. Discourage your members from the temptation to show up at the event with placards and slogans that would try to "correct" other people's orientation to the environment. Those behaviors will only alienate people from the gospel. Allow this to be a positive time of public cooperation and affirmation.

40. Resources for Tending Creation

Following are several Christian-produced resources for your information and interest. Scores of wonderful secular publications and organizations are working to help citizens be better caretakers of the environment. We encourage you to visit your local library and discover the helpful resources available.

ORGANIZATIONS

CHRISTIAN ENVIRONMENTAL ASSOCIATION
P.O. Box 15026
Fremont, CA 94539
This group will provide you with expert help to "green your church." They also sponsor cross-cultural trips to pristine environmental areas, offer college-level courses on the environment and host weekend workshops on the environment for churches and colleges.

BOOKS
Environmental Stewardship by Ruth Goring Stewart (InterVarsity, 1990).
This is a collection of six Bible studies on the call for Christians to care for creation.
How to Rescue the Earth Without Worshipping Nature by Tony Campolo (Thomas Nelson, 1992).
A video version of the book is available through Thomas Nelson's video division.
Fifty Ways You Can Help Save the Planet by Tony Campolo and Gordon Aeschliman (InterVarsity, 1992).

CURRICULUM
Reclaiming the Garden by Randy Peterson, (David C. Cook, 1992).
This is a four-session study on the environment. A workbook and video are included.

VI.
THE SICK
Serving the Afflicted

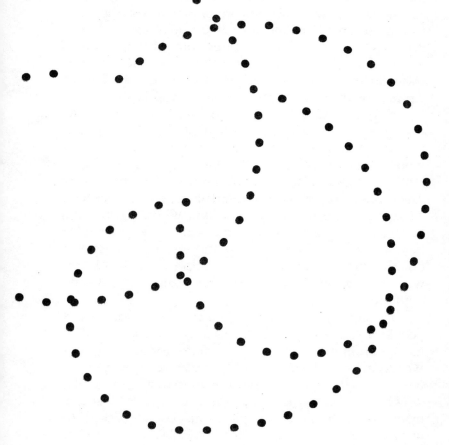

Think back to the days when you were just a child in Sunday School. It seems like half of the stories we remember about Jesus were His encounters with the sick: the woman who touches His gown; the blind man calling from the side of the road; the Roman leader pleading for his daughter; the man lowered through the roof; Lazarus; the lepers. Jesus couldn't pass up a sick person. The famous "missionary" verse, "Ask the Lord of the harvest, therefore, to send out workers into his harvest field" (Matt. 9:38) is actually the prayer of Christ after going through several towns and villages healing "every disease and sickness" (Matt. 9:35). Jesus tells us that one way to recognize His disciples is by their behavior—they visit the sick.

Sickness comes at several levels. It can simply be a temporary nuisance or it can permanently immobilize. The Church should be particularly concerned about people whose lives are permanently altered due to health problems. All kinds of modern afflictions affect millions of Americans each year: cancer, heart failure, Multiple Sclerosis, AIDS and epilepsy, to name a few. When we lose our health, we are constantly feeling a "deficit." Something has been taken from us, we cannot muster up the energy to do our work, we cannot perform simple duties that before were unconscious activities, we cannot laugh without wincing from the pain.

Sometimes illness brings about a change in relationships: people are not too sure how to act around us, so they avoid us. We are not a natural pick anymore for the night out. We experience deep depression and a sense of uselessness. It is as though our dignity disappeared with our health.

When Europe experienced the Great Black Plague, as many as one third of all people on that continent died. An unusually large percentage of those were Christians. Historians tell us why—not so much as an explanation, but rather as a mystery. Apparently, while citizens were packing their goods and fleeing to other towns in order to avoid the Plague, Christians stayed behind to care for the sick. This was not a form of simple charity. It was an invitation to death—contact with the Plague was fatal. So Christians died in large numbers as they ushered the sick into their eternal reward.

That kind of commitment is astounding. Would Christians today do the same? Could we find it within ourselves to pay the same price? That is a tough question to answer. Thank God few of us will have to face that dilemma. The modern-day challenge to care for the sick is not so costly.

As Christian leaders, we must demonstrate the way of compassion today. This suggests we take on the pain and cries of those who live with chronic illness. It means not avoiding those we would rather not be around. It means serving the afflicted even when a cost is involved.

It is Christian to weep when others weep. And, in this sense, society could use a few more tears, and we think they should come from the Church.

41. Show Compassion to Modern Lepers

"Unclean! Unclean! Unclean!" In Jesus' time, shouts and ringing bells warned people that lepers were approaching. "Clear the way! Don't get close enough to touch them or you yourself may become infected. It will eat your body, and you will die before your days are meant to end." Yet Jesus held the hands of lepers. He touched, He soothed, He comforted.

Today, an outstanding woman emulates Jesus' model closely. Around the world she is admired, almost worshiped. Wherever she travels, people rush to her and stretch to touch her hand. "Mama! Mama!" they call out. Mother Teresa, friend of the world. Why does she garner so much love and admiration? She is a friend to the leper. She gave up her citizenship to become a permanent resident of India, where her mission was to care for the "least of these." Calcutta, a giant city that portrays so perfectly the human tragedy, became home to the Mother of Mercy. Sounds a bit like Jesus, doesn't it?

And what about the latest version of leprosy—AIDS? It is hard to find a Mother Teresa here. No selfless angel of Jesus to capture the imagination and hearts of hardened reporters, cynical humanists and, yes, judgmental Christians. Unfortunately, the Church has largely denounced the modern lepers. "Thank God we are not like them!" seems to be our rallying cry. Some have gone so far as to say, "Well, they are getting what they deserve!"

It does no good to point fingers. We are all to blame. We are losing this battle. If we continue on our current path, we won't go down as angels of mercy who stayed behind to contract the Black Plague. We won't leave an endearing impression of little Mother Teresas.

Our compassion in the days ahead needs to be a measure of our repentance. We pray that God will raise hundreds of Christian leaders who will call their congregations to step inside the painful world of people with AIDS. Here are several places to begin:

- The most important step is putting aside our pride and judgment. The Holy Spirit must renew our minds and heal our prejudices.

- The next step is to become practical. Look up AIDS groups in your community. Inquire where they meet and where the sick are living. Express your interest in doing whatever you can to soften the blows life has dealt them. You do not need to express your desire to do this "as a Christian"—the opportunity to mention that may come later. Do it simply as someone who cares.

- If an AIDS hospice is located in your
  community, make the rounds. Again,
  we would emphasize that you do not
  do it as a church official, but as one who
  wants to quietly serve. Ask the hospice
  staff for advice on what you can do.
  They are experienced and will be glad
  to show you the way.

42. Establish a "SickNet"

Sometimes we are caught off guard by a friend's account
of what it was like to be sick for the previous month—
loneliness, isolation, depression, lost income, stacked-up
work. Usually, our response is, "Oh, I wish I had known!"

Where do people turn when they need the help? Who is
ready to give extra help to make their illness a little more
tolerable? Who is there to take care of the details that cannot afford to slip? Some people feel awkward depending
on others; they fear they will be a burden. Yet most people
are more than willing to lend a hand—if only they knew
who needed help.

Here are some suggestions for ensuring that the sick
people in your congregation get cared for:

- Ask members to help create a "SickNet"—a
  simple system to make sure people who are
  sick do not go unnoticed.

- Establish a second level of volunteers who
  would be willing to sign up for a minimal
  weekly commitment (or as needs arise). These
  people will perform simple tasks to relieve the
  sick person's burden: cook a meal or two,
  spend an hour cleaning the house or running a
  few errands. You would also want to find a

couple of people who would like to
take on prayer duty—visiting the sick
specifically to pray for them.

Here is how the system works: If someone gets sick, he
or she calls the church office (or a fellow church member
calls in). The call is forwarded to the designated coordina-
tor of the week, who finds out what the needs are. From the
roster of volunteers, people are contacted to help meet a
specific need. The sick person's name is also added to that
week's prayer chain.

You might also put this system to work for people outside the church. Ask members to be on the lookout for
neighbors, coworkers and acquaintances who are not a
part of the church. Emphasize that this program is for *everyone*, not just for close friends and Sunday School class members. Imagine the impact when a sick mother (who is not
a church member) receives a hot meal to feed herself and
her three kids. What a statement of love and compassion!

If your SickNet branches out beyond your church, be
prepared for more ministry. You may find that you have
been put in touch with dozens of people who have little
history with church or Christ. Of course, these kinds of
opportunities are what we pray for. The idea is just to be
sure you are mentally and physically prepared for a much
larger scope of caring than a few errands and meals.

43. Support the Families

Sick people need help, but so do their family members. One
of life's sad statistics is the impact of serious illness on families. Only 10 percent of marriages survive an illness where
one of the partners is bedridden or immobilized for a pro-
tracted period of time. The stress upon the other spouse to
survive financially, manage the household affairs, raise the

children and plan for the future is apparently too much. Whereas home used to be that place of shelter, relaxation and rest, now it is an emotional and physical drain.

It is not our place to judge people who cannot survive these circumstances. But it is our place, as Christian leaders, to ask what our churches could do to support these stressed-out families.

Few churches have more than two or three couples experiencing this trauma. Our suggestion is that you look for qualified volunteers who can attach themselves to these families and actively search out ways to be useful and supportive. Volunteers can help with housecleaning, doctor visits, shopping and yard work. Think of ways to free up the spouse for those essential family activities, such as playing with the kids, attending to the partner, getting away for some rest time and going to favorite church or community events. These are the most important elements of family life, and they are always the first to go when crisis hits.

You may want to branch out to other people in the community. Take referrals from church members who want to be involved in supporting their neighbors who may have this need. Encourage the creation of a team around each family. This would ensure a much more consistent style of service and would help prevent burnout for the care providers.

44. Go to the Sick

We mentioned earlier the loneliness that often accompanies those who are sick. This is especially true of people who are confined to long-term care facilities. Perhaps they are unable to care for themselves or they may have a sickness that requires constant attention from medical staff. Whatever the cause, their life is lived away from the normal environment of family laughter, kitchen aromas, favorite possessions and rooms with emotional histories.

Most cities have several centers for people with long-term illnesses. Our suggestion is that you set up a volunteer corps of church members who will become familiar with one of these centers. The key to this idea is implementing a regular routine that becomes part of the weekly schedule for people in these facilities. We know a church that has a dozen adults and many youth who spend a few hours after church each Sunday at one of these centers. The kids talk with people and establish friendships. Adults run errands and make sure everyone has what they need. Birthdays, holidays and other special days are celebrated, so no one feels left out or forgotten.

These church members always end their Sunday visits with lunch together at a local family restaurant. This service is not just good for those in the center, it clearly binds these Christians together in a deeper bond of love and camaraderie. Children learn that taking specific steps of charity is both biblical and fun. The modeling by adults achieves much more than any sermon or teaching on compassion. It makes good sense to tie these ideas of "church" together.

And who knows what kind of angel we are attending. A good chunk of our New Testament comes to us through a man who was able to finish the manuscript because of a church that sent a helper during a prolonged stretch of illness.

45. Give to the Sick

People who are sick are often hesitant to ask for help, even when they are connected to a caring church. That response is understandable: they want to preserve their dignity, and they do not want to feel like a burden.

A church in Chicago is sensitive to this situation. They came up with a great plan that any church could implement. The pastor announced a special meeting for members who would be willing to give a few hours a month for friends and neighbors who were sick. He worked hard to sell the meeting because he believed he was on to something good. A couple dozen people showed up. They all brought along crayons, colored pens, scissors and tape, as they were instructed to do. The pastor stood at a blackboard and asked members to shout out things they wish they could ask people to do for them when sick. They came up with a list that included mowing the lawn, running errands, cooking a meal and taking the kids to their sports practices.

Here is what they did with the ideas. The pastor asked everyone to think through 12 activities they would be willing to do throughout the year for someone who is sick— one activity a month. Each volunteer then made up 12 special coupons on poster paper, each coupon describing a specific service they would be happy to perform. The volunteer's name and phone number were included.

All of the coupons were collected, shuffled and arranged into packets of 12 (a volunteer appeared no more than once in each packet). Members made colorful envelopes for each of the coupon sets. The church's phone number and address were included on the holder.

These packets (a couple dozen in all) were stored in the church office. As the church received calls regarding people who were experiencing serious illness, one of these packets was sent with the regular visitation team that was already in place. At the end of the visit, the packet was handed over as a gift from the church. The volunteers said they found the unsuspecting phone calls (to redeem coupons) a refreshing break from the normal routine of the month, and it did not seem burdensome because the services were varied and infrequent. The idea has grown to the point that several packets are in the church office waiting to be used. And as you might surmise, many of the recovered people wanted to check out this church that sent 12 cheerful volunteers their way.

46. Spread the Vision for Serving the Sick

Choose a Sunday on your annual church calendar to focus on the importance of caring for the sick. Here are some of the things you could do that day:

- Have the sermon and Sunday School teaching center on the theme of caring for those who are sick.

- Create a special time of prayer for people who are presently ill. Think through creative ways to involve all the members in a circle of prayer during the service.

- Ask a member of your congregation who has experienced chronic illness to give a short presentation on how to care for people in that situation. It is helpful to simply remind people there are specific things that can be done.

- Ask staff at the local long-term care center to make a presentation to the church on what members can do to bring warmth and cheer to those who are shut in.

- Organize a Saturday or Sunday afternoon seminar for those who would like to pursue care of the sick further.

- You could use this Sunday as an opportunity to implement the idea we suggested regarding care coupons. Members could pray ahead of time regarding how many coupons they would be willing to offer over the next 12 months. Have little cards in the offering for people to fill out. You could tally these cards and report to the congregation before the end of the ser-

vice how many coupons the church will
be distributing to the sick that year.

47. Resources for Helping the Afflicted

These are the best resources we know to help you in your
ministry to the sick. No doubt you will discover additional
local resources as you implement steps of caring.

ORGANIZATIONS

AIDS RESOURCE MINISTRY
12488 Venice Blvd.
Los Angeles, CA 90066

HEALTH MINISTRIES ASSOCIATION
2427 Country Lane
Poland, OH 44514

NURSES CHRISTIAN FELLOWSHIP
P.O. Box 7895
Madison, WI 53707

BOOKS

Christian Caregiving: A Way of Life by
Kenneth Haugk (Augsburg, 1984).
*The Healing Power of Doing Good:
The Health and Spiritual Benefits of Helping
Others* by Allan Luke and Peggy Payne
(Ballantine, 1991).
Spiritual Care by Judith Shelley and Sharon
Fish (InterVarsity, 1988).
This resource is invaluable for nurses who
want to understand how to bring their spiri-
tual values to the job. The companion Bible

study section will help church members understand how better to serve the sick.

MAGAZINE

Journal of Christian Nursing
P.O. Box 1400
Downers Grove, IL 60515

CURRICULUM

Called to Care
United Church Resources
800 North Third St.
St. Louis, MO 63102
This ambitious handbook has 52 sections on caring. Approximately half of them concern health issues. Excellent further resources are included.

Caring People Bible Studies
(InterVarsity, 1991).
This series of eight Bible study booklets provides biblical ideas and practical suggestions on how to care for people with health problems.

VII.
PRISONERS
Befriending the Outcast

S it back for a moment and imagine life behind bars. A home the size of a van—shared with a stranger. No private bath or toilet. Outdoor activities restricted to a rigid routine and mostly on a cement slab. A line to use the telephone, and no number for people to call back. Recreation time limited to prescribed hours in full public scrutiny. Meals served cafeteria style. No garage for hobbies, no dog to chase the stick, no kids to swing over the shoulder.

That is the pretty part of the picture.

Add fear. Add the loneliness of being completely removed from anyone who cares about you. Add physical harm that includes beatings and gang rape. Add the loss of respect and dignity, the inability to provide for a family and the vulnerability of wondering if the special loved one will slip into the life of another. Add the prison record to the résumé, the inability to vote again (if incarcerated for a felony)—losing the basic right of citizenship. Add the pure impotence of not being able to make anything of your life.

Some people live this way because of a couple days' experimentation with drugs. Others because of a joyride in someone else's car or a $50 heist that went awry and left someone dead. And still others because of cold-blooded, premeditated murder.

What does it say about our society that we have lost the patience and care to ensure the correctional system continues to treat offenders as human beings? That we have lost the desire to separate those who made a judgment error once from those who engaged in torture for sport? That we have found it easier to lock people away into a man-made hell than to accept the hard work of rehabilitating them?

At this moment, more black Americans are entering prison than entering college. Do we honestly believe this is an acceptable measure of "what blacks are like" or do we just not care?

Christians are uniquely equipped to stand in the gap of justice for our nation's prisoners. We ourselves have not been dealt with according to our sins; we have experienced the mercy of Calvary—not because we are reformed, but because we could not reform ourselves; we continue to commit sins against others and God—malice, deceit and immorality—but we continually experience a patient God who woos us back to the right path with the compassion of a perfectly loving parent.

Furthermore, Christians are able to care about those in prison because we have our own rich heritage of prison life. Our Lord went to prison and stood trial. He was executed. His disciples experienced floggings and early deaths. Thousands of first-century Christians were tortured in government prisons (for breaking civil laws), and hundreds of thousands since have died behind bars far removed from their loved ones. At this very moment, thousands of Christians around the world are in prison awaiting a judge's decision on their future. Their circumstances are no better than the image we painted at the beginning of this chapter.

Christians care about those in prison because our God is just and fair. We know in our hearts that much of the prison system is evil, going beyond the boundaries of punishment and rehabilitation. The abuse experienced by many prisoners is a crime against humanity and God. We do not honestly believe that anyone deserves those conditions. But it all seems so overwhelming, doesn't it? What can one person do? Fortunately, several excellent organizations will help us focus our care on both the prisoner and the prison system. It is downright Christian to love the prisoner, and we strongly encourage you and your church to show prisoners God's redeeming love.

48. Advocate for Change

The idea of "advocacy" is central to the Christian experience. We have one who speaks to the Father on our behalf—an advocate. Our understanding of grace is just this: Jesus voluntarily took on our penalty, and now He asks the Judge to release us from the sentence.

We need to right our thinking regarding the prison system. Christians cannot in good conscience ignore the dehumanizing and cruel approach toward offenders that far exceeds our sensibilities of what is just. We have three suggestions for ways you could lead your church to advocate on behalf of the prisoner:

- Link up with the Association for Public Justice and Prison Fellowship for ideas. Both of these Christian organizations have done the hard work of researching specific legislation on prison reform. Ask them for information on how your church could make a difference.

- Contact Amnesty International, a secular watchdog group, for information about letter-writing campaigns to governments around the world. This group researches prison abuses throughout the world without regard to political orientation. They have a first-rate track record for identifying specific prisoners of conscience and then mobilizing a virtual flood of international mail to both lawmakers and government leaders demanding the release of those unjustly incarcerated. Amnesty International has also been successful in influencing governments to implement proper procedures for bringing alleged offenders to trial, establishing fair sentencing scales and upgrading prison conditions.

- Advocate at the local level. We have Christian friends who live in the inner city of Los Angeles. They have seen all too often how youths who enter juvenile hall end up on the fast track to a professional life of crime. Because these Christians live in the city, they often know offending youths by name. When they come up for a hearing, these Christians go to the courtroom and ask the judge to have the children put in their custody. The case is made that they are neighbors, they understand the pressures, and they are linked to businesses that are willing to give these youths after-school employment to keep them off the streets and teach them a useful skill. The judges usually grant the request because they understand the brutality of the prison system as well as anyone. It makes sense for the Church to take on this advocacy role. And it reminds us in a physical manner of the One who advocates for us.

49. Become a Pro

You may want to take advantage of excellent training resources available to Christian leaders. The needs of prison ministry are so immense that it is possible to lose heart and "leave it up to the professionals." If you are a full-time pastor, your church may encourage you to take study leaves or continuing education courses; use some of those hours to learn about prison ministry. Or if there are people in your church who seem to be strongly interested in this type of service, urge them to lead a program to connect with prisoners.

Prison Fellowship has developed two key training programs. The first is an undergraduate-level course that is taught by staff who are based in your area. The course lasts 20 hours, and you can qualify for two continuing education units through Trinity College in Deerfield, Illinois. The second is a graduate-level course that is self-directed. This one is designed specifically for pastors and other Christian leaders and is listed as an independent study course at Trinity Evangelical Divinity School.

If the Lord is putting it on your heart to take some significant steps toward caring for prisoners and leading your congregation into this area of need, then these courses would be well worth the time. Why not ask for a special study leave to take on the challenge? We do not believe the Church has done enough to reach out to prisoners, so we are enthusiastic when quality resources like these are available to help leaders chart the course.

50. Support Prisoners' Families

Work with your congregation to find ways to support the families of persons in prison. The needs will vary considerably. One family may be struggling with the problem of a child in juvenile detention. Parents of these troubled youths face tremendous stress as they consider the future of their child and how painful life has become for their "little" one.

Another family may have to deal with the loss of the primary breadwinner. This is both an emotional and material loss. We have met pastors who have a program to convince landlords not to evict the families of recently imprisoned persons. The church guarantees an aggressive search to help other family members find employment to make up for the loss.

Identify families in your community who are experiencing these kinds of losses. If your church is part of a denomination, go through the chaplain. Otherwise you work with a local ministerial fellowship. Here are some steps you could take:

- Ask the family of a prisoner to explain to the church the kinds of hardships it experiences Ask them to offer specific advice on what you can do to help.

- Provide practical support to families that have a member in prison. Perhaps they need help with errands, job hunting, skills development, public assistance or education. When possible, intervene with landlords and creditors who could extend a little more time to help recover from the initial loss of a wage earner.

- Encourage the children of prisoners to join the church youth group or children's program. And make sure they receive a warm welcome. Involve them in fun and fulfilling activities in the church and community. This will keep them from the sensation of being cut off (due to the stigma of prison) and may prevent "acting out" that leads to juvenile crimes.

- Offer marriage and family counseling. The stress of imprisonment upon marriages is almost unmatched. Long-term incarceration usually leads to divorce. Professional assistance from qualified Christian counselors could keep families together. The temporary loss of a spouse or parent is harsh enough. The permanent loss of family is a cruel addition to the sentence.

51. Correspond with Those in Prison

You may be able to round up some support from your congregation to write letters to people in prison. Prisoners often request correspondence to combat their loneliness. Many offenders are shipped to prisons far from their families and have no contact with friends for their entire sentence. And a lot of friends drop away in time.

You probably have people in your congregation who cannot expend a lot of energy on work projects or missions' trips, but they do want to minister in some capacity. They may have a patient, tender disposition and a love for prayer. Recruit some of these people to create a fellowship of letter writers. This idea is not so complex; here are a few things you could line up:

- Collect names and addresses of prisoners who would like correspondence. You could get these names through Prison Fellowship or Sojourners magazine (your library may carry it).

- Recruit people who will make a minimal commitment, perhaps one letter a month. Hold an initial kickoff session where everyone writes their first letter.

- As you receive responses to the correspondence, pray together for these people who have to live away from their families and in conditions that are less than dignifying.

- Each month, pray for some of these contacts during the church service. A unified congregational prayer is a wonderful way to support a prisoner.

- Encourage your correspondence team to offer Bible study materials to the prisoners. Those who have a relationship with the Lord will appreciate your sensitivity in helping them grow spiritually. Others, who may never have taken a step toward Christ, may find the awful life of prison a nudge toward God. One word of caution: The intention should be to truly love and befriend prisoners, not necessarily "win their souls" (although that would be wonderful). They are likely to be turned off if they sense your letters are merely a method of evangelism.

- In time, your pen pal may introduce you to their family. Offer tangible support through the church. Perhaps your denomination has a fellowship in the same region where the family lives. See if you can encourage that fellowship to follow through with practical steps of support.

52. Go to the Prisoner

Most churches are located within driving distance of at least a county jail. We recommend that you encourage church members to volunteer for a regular visitation program. Ask the prison chaplain for help if you are not sure how best to begin. We sometimes have the image of prisoners as people who are hardened, cynical or even animal-like. However, the majority of them wish they were not in their situation and enjoy contact with people who are willing to take the time to brighten their day.

If you have a juvenile hall within driving distance, consider involving your high school youth in a regular sports program. It is good for your youth to accept these young prisoners as equals and to learn the art of regular caring. It is also good for them to see that unwise actions can lead to a lot of pain. If your church is located near a university or college, take advantage of Christian fellowship groups. Inspire these students to include a sports event at a juvenile facility as part of their weekly routine. Doing something as a group is not too threatening for most college students. It is a natural "in" and can be the first step toward helping youth stay away from the life of crime once the sentence is complete.

53. Give to the Prisoner

We know a church in Southern California that thought big when asking the question, What can we give to prisoners this Christmas?

As they brainstormed various possibilities, they got the nutty idea that they should do something for every prisoner in Chino State Penitentiary. "What's so big about that?" you ask. Chino has *17,000* inmates—more than the average university has students. And that church has approximately 2,500 members.

Here is what they did: In the month preceding Christmas, church members began to bake cookies by the dozens. Home ovens and the church's commercial ovens went into full-time use. The children at the church's school made hundreds of small gifts. And the adults and parents wrote cards of greeting—not just "sign-off" notes but actual sit-down-and-read-this, handwritten letters. Finally, a fund drive was implemented to purchase Bibles in modern language.

On Christmas Day, 17,000 *dozen* homemade cookies, 17,000 handmade crafts, 17,000 personal letters and 17,000 Bibles were distributed to the inmates. Now that is a *big* labor of love! And it was not a one-time event. This has become an annual event for the church.

We encourage churches to match the idea (on a smaller scale perhaps) and feel the energy of all levels of the church working together to remind prisoners that somebody loves them.

54. Spread the Vision for Prison Ministry

Select a particular Sunday on your church calendar to be the day your church focuses on the needs of prisoners. Here are a few items that might be included:

- Plan the Sunday service around the theme of the prisoner. Highlight the biblical passages that call for justice and tell the stories of prisoners we learn about in Scripture (at least a dozen examples can be used, including the apostle Paul).

- Ask your Sunday School teachers to include the biblical call to care for prisoners in that week's lesson.

- Include a bulletin insert on the state of prisoners around the world. Prison Fellowship could provide you with materials.

- Ask the local prison chaplain to do a presentation on what Christians can do locally.

- Spend time in prayer for prisoners.

- Ask a family of prisoners to share their story. Ask them for specific advice on how to care for the families of prisoners.

- Offer a Saturday or Sunday afternoon seminar for those who want to learn more about prison ministry.

- If your church would like to implement the idea of providing prisoners with Christmas gifts, this could be the Sunday to tell the story of Chino State Penitentiary and see if some members would like to run with the idea. If you have an active youth group, the idea could catch on if adapted to the needs of youth in juvenile detention.

55. Resources for Working with Prisoners

ORGANIZATIONS

AMNESTY INTERNATIONAL
322 Eighth Ave.
New York, NY 10001

ASSOCIATION FOR PUBLIC JUSTICE
321 8th Street, NE
Washington, DC 20002

PRISON FELLOWSHIP
P.O. Box 17500
Washington, DC 20041
Without question, this is the premier organization to contact for help with working with prisoners. They offer several resources:

- *Jubilee*, a newsletter that will keep you current on the world of prison ministry and encourage you to keep at it.

- *Tips for Teachers*, a quarterly publication for people who want to lead Bible studies in prison.

- A certified training course (20 hours of class time) offered to leaders—Trinity College grants two continuing education units upon certification.

- A self-directed graduate course in prison ministry through Trinity Evangelical Divinity

School. The content was designed by
Prison Fellowship, and the course is good
for two graduate units.

BOOKS
Convicted by Chuck Colson and Daniel
Van Ness (Good News, 1989).
Crime and Its Victims by Daniel Van Ness
(InterVarsity, 1986).
Life Sentence by Chuck Colson
(Revell, 1981).

VIII.
THE ELDERLY
Honoring the Wise

Proverbs speaks of silver hair as the crown of life, the distinguishing mark of wisdom (see Prov. 16:31). Something went awfully wrong between the time when Proverbs was written and our modern society. The pace of these silver-crowned folk is too slow for our fast-paced lifestyles, so we shove them aside. Their presence is a chore, so we leave them in remote homes. They remind us of our own mortality, so we look the other way when they come near. They draw very little respect from our generation—it is as though they should be ashamed to have "declined" into old age.

But this attitude toward the elderly is utterly foolish! These people bring to us generations of wisdom, stories of global progress and decline, memories of a time before TV, cars, airplanes, moon launches and nuclear bombs. They chart for us the childlike steps of nations determined to be modern, of despots grabbing power, of people trying to be free, of frontiers becoming urban centers. They link together long-dead generations and today's infant. They see life, they see death, they hear music, they hear nothing.

And often our minds and lives are so cluttered with going and getting that we miss it all. Yes, we certainly miss the untapped gold mine in the rocking chair.

When we ignore the elderly, we are more than fools, we are coldhearted and callous. What kind of society measures worth by production output? What kind of people gauge value by mobility and dexterity? What kind of nation measures "human" by "returns"? Think about the waning years of the elderly—all the years they have lived now stored up in their frame; all the people they have known; cities they have built; wars they have fought; fields they have planted; droughts they have survived; children they have birthed and perhaps buried; frontiers they have settled; and moments they have experienced that changed the course of the ages.

Many of the elderly remain active and sharp in their final years, but unfortunately, for all too many of the elderly, the waning years are painful and even bitter—they sit to catch their breath, strain to hear the question, squint to see the bird, and stutter in response to "tea or coffee?" The moments are not so kind on their minds—confusing yesterday's news with today's soap opera. The sun sets much slower than they recall of old and children play at war like there never really was one. And family pushes them aside to the chair in the corner like some vase Aunt Elda gave them 20 Christmases ago.

It is strange to reflect how "pro-life" Christians often claim to be—defending lives that have yet to see a sunrise, while discarding those that have seen a thousand times 30. The gravity and dignity of one so tempered by the ages is missed by our hectic pace and flagrant clamoring for more. If the integrity of our pro-life commitments is measured by the scale of honoring our elderly, then we are not doing so well.

We believe that Christians need to steer society back toward giving the elderly the love and respect they deserve. Our world is unable to distinguish the value of the flickering ember over the Hollywood dream of forever young. We need to return to the days when silver hair was a crown, when children and adults alike sat at the feet of grandma and grandpa to learn from their wisdom. This is a Christian duty, and leaders need to set the course.

56. Record the Stories

One way to confer dignity on the elderly is to ask them to help assemble our history—to tell the stories of the past and to help us learn how we are connected to the generations before us.

The very act of adults sitting at the feet of the elderly goes beyond any words we could articulate. What an example to our children! We want to stress, though, that it would be counterproductive to use this opportunity to make a point to the youth. We already have made our point and it does not speak well of our respect for the elderly. Rather than design venues "for the kids' benefit," we need to structure times with the elderly that help us, as adults, regain our admiration for them. And, of course, we involve the children in the process so they can benefit as well. Here are a few of the activities you could plan:

- Create some theme evenings. One example would be "Our House." Ask the elderly to describe their homes of old. Involve adults or youth to draw the plan of the house as it is described. List the appliances and utilities that make a house operate. Then draw a contrasting picture of our current homes. Other themes could be transportation, technology, kids' games, work. The idea is to get the older folks talking and sharing their memories.

- Ask those who have lived in your town or community for many years to tell what it was like "way back when." Ask them to paint a verbal picture of life in "the good ol' days." Arrange a four-stop tour through the town where they explain what used to be there and what did not. (We recently heard the story from a person who remembers when Los Angeles International Airport was just one small tin shed and a landing strip).

- Ask the elderly to talk about family. Plot out their family tree on a blackboard beginning as far back as they can remember—where they were from, what they did for a living, who were their children, and so on. You will develop a fascinating sense of being just a few breaths away from famous events, such as the Civil War.

57. Work for the Elderly

Many of the elderly in your church are still living in their own homes. They maintain wonderful gardens, enjoy their hobbies and keep up with the repairs.

But it does become more difficult over time to maintain these habits. Slowly but surely, some tasks have to be let go as some things become too difficult and strenuous. And it can be depressing to see the house slip: the oranges on the top branches rot, the hedge does not carry the same square trim, the weeds are equal to the grass and the variety of flowers diminishes.

It makes a lot of sense for church members to pick up some of the slack for the elderly of their congregations. And it should always be done in an environment of dignity. The way to proceed is simple: Gather a trusty group of adults and youth who would like to volunteer for a few hours each week. Get the word out through the congregation that these eager beavers are ready. Explain that you would like to take on regular routines such as garden care and housecleaning as well as fix-it projects, such as a broken lock, a cracked window or dripping faucets.

If your church is small, you will probably be able to manage all of these without much more than word of mouth. If the task gets too large, create a way for the elderly to request help. Write up those requests on index cards, complete with name and phone number, and post them on a bulletin board expressly for the elderly. The group of volunteers can check the board regularly and take those cards that they will handle.

If you find the system is working well and enough energy is going around to expand the idea, consider broadening the program to elderly folk who are not a part of the church. They are not as likely to be attached to a group or club that would offer this kind of help, and it makes a lot of sense that the church would be there to stand in the gap. Be careful not to do this in order to "get your testimony in sideways." That would belittle your assistance and in a way trap the poor soul to listen to your sermon (work in exchange for listening). In fact, you may hear a lot about what is wrong with religious folk before you receive permission to say what you think is right with them.

58. Provide a Real Home

Convalescent centers exist for good reasons. Some people have reached a physical state where their only good option for medical attention is in a professionally operated center. It is right and appropriate to avail ourselves of this help when it is needed. But sometimes older folks end up in these homes because their options run out. They are left with no family, they are unable to manage their large home, they need a little assistance with certain tasks—but no one is available to care for them.

Your church can provide a wonderful service for people in this circumstance. Many of your members are at that stage where the nest is empty and the house is just a little too quiet. A few extra bedrooms get dusted every so often but otherwise remain untouched. Find out from your members if any of them would be interested in inviting an elderly person to move in. You could create a small care group of such members, because similar issues and needs are sure to emerge among the "home providers." Some older people are perfectly independent; all they need is a place to stay. Others require more care, and some provisions may need to be made—a ramp for easy access to the house, certain medical equipment, special foods for dietary needs.

Ask local welfare officials how funds that these folk would have spent on a convalescent center could be used toward home care. Many federal and state programs allow for a day nurse—someone who comes into the home to provide for certain meals, physical checkups and ablution duties. By having some extra help, you will be freed up to focus on the friendship and create an atmosphere of welcome and warmth.

The likelihood that these folks will be able to enjoy church is much higher as you include them in your activities and transport them to special events of their choice. You may also consider opening up your home once a week for low-key activities aimed at their pleasure—card games, tea and quilting.

59. Go to the Elderly

Chances are, your town has a convalescent center where dozens of people do not receive regular visits from family. In our experience, these centers are sensitive to their members and would be more than happy to suggest who you could befriend.

We recommend that you enlist a group of volunteers who would be willing to visit people at least once a week and always on the same schedule. Elderly folk like to anticipate that regular event the same way we look forward to certain pleasurable activities. Try to find a team that includes a variety of ages—older adults, middle-aged and children. Communication happens at several levels.

Children are especially valuable to the elderly. Unfortunately, kids are often cut off from them. Our society is so uneasy with the vision of growing old that we tend to protect our children. We think we are doing them a favor, but in fact we are teaching them not to respect our elders and to fear old age. It is not fair to the elderly either. If you have included children in these kinds of routines, then you know the delight they bring—the hugs, the hand holding, the laughter, the stories recounting younger years. What a gift! Be sure to orient your children initially to the environment. They may not be prepared for the spontaneous manner of some older folk, who may reach out to hug them. Tell the kids it is okay to hug back.

Some kids will have their first experience with death in this context. We know of kids who insisted on going to the funerals of friends they had made in the convalescent center. Yes, the experience was traumatic. That is the nature of life. And death is part of life. Learning to grieve in youth is good and fair.

You may want to include pets in some of your visits. Many convalescent centers are actually requesting this service. Friendly dogs and cats bring back good memories for many people whose last household companion was a pet. Animals love the attention. It is not every day they can receive hugs and strokes for several hours. Check with your center for their specific guidelines. You may discover your town has a special service just for this. In some cities, it is called the "Pet Parade." These organizations provide pets that are trained to give and receive love and affection. You can "check them out" for a regular routine of visitation.

60. Give to the Elderly

A small farming town in the Northwest has found a wonderful way to involve children in giving to the elderly. The town has one school and one convalescent center.

Everyone seems to know everyone in this community. A warm relationship exists between the school and the center, and many of the school kids have relatives living in the center. The town developed a way to bring these groups closer together.

The lower grades are typical of any school; they do crafts every other day, or so it seems. These crafts serve as a good learning tool in creativity, but unfortunately, they are usually tossed out at the end of the week, if not the end of the day. On special occasions such as Thanksgiving, Christmas and Valentine's Day, the crafts get a little more extravagant, but they too hit the basket before long. What a waste.

But this school came up with a creative solution: On holidays and other special days, the kids in the lower grades make cards and crafts for the folks in the convalescent center. Each time, the kids are given an orientation to the elderly: What do you suppose an elderly person who lives up there on the hill would like to receive on Valentine's Day? Children have a natural capacity to love, and they catch on quickly to the types of messages they can send. The convalescent center is a wonderful sight on these special days, and the elderly truly appreciate the thought.

If your town has a convalescent home, we suggest you follow this little town's lead. If your church has its own school, that would be the most natural place to start. And, if possible, let the kids deliver the cards and crafts. If you do not have a church-sponsored school, join the PTA and volunteer as a parent to work with teachers to implement this idea.

61. Spread the Vision for Honoring the Wise

Choose a day on your church calendar to focus on the Christian service of caring for the elderly. Here are a few things you could do on that day:

- Plan the Sunday service on the theme of caring for the elderly (remember, the father and mother of our faith were quite old when they received their first child).

- Ask all the Sunday School teachers to include the theme of the elderly in that week's lesson.

- Invite some people from the convalescent center to make a presentation in church on special ways to care for the elderly.

- If your church has any elderly folk as regular members, ask them to take a large role in that Sunday service—singing, giving a testimony, praying or telling a story.

- If anyone in your church has become involved with the elderly in a special way, this would be a good time to have them tell what they do. Perhaps they would provide some inspiration for others who are considering working with the elderly.

- Hold a special time of prayer for the elderly. Pray for people by name.

- Offer a special Saturday or Sunday afternoon seminar for church members who would like to learn more about caring for the elderly.

62. Resources for Caring for the Elderly

BOOKS
Caring for Your Aging Parents
by Barbara Deane (NavPress, 1989).

Getting Ready for a Great Retirement by
Barbara Deane (NavPress, 1991).
Life and Death Decisions by Robert O. Orr,
David Schiedermayer, David Biebel
(NavPress, 1990).
As Our Years Increase by Tim Stafford
(Zondervan, 1989).
This book is out of print—check it out at
your library—a great resource.
From Here to Retirement by Paul Brown
(WORD, 1988).

VIDEO

Maturity Without Mercy
(WORD, 1993).

IX.
THE IMMIGRANT
Helping Those New to Our Land

Much of the recorded history of our faith concerns people who were aliens, strangers in a strange land. Abraham was called by God to leave his homeland and go to a place God would show him. There, among strangers, he set up his new home. His grandson, an alien in his own way, worked 14 years for an uncle in a distant land, then settled back down on the home place, only to lose his favorite son to the schemes of wicked siblings.

Joseph grew up an alien in Pharaoh's prisons and then his court. A drought forced Joseph's brothers to join him (see Gen. 46:6), and in time they became the despised and enslaved aliens who worshiped a strange God. It would be 400 years before they were able to escape and settle in the land of Canaan. It did not end there, as captivity ensued several times until the coming of Christ.

Israel clearly understood what it meant to be alien. And God regularly called them to be kind and hospitable to the foreigner: "Do not oppress an alien; you yourselves know how it feels to be aliens, because you were aliens in Egypt" (Exod. 23:9).

The New Testament carries this theme forward. Jesus told us we will always be aliens in the land. And Peter echoed this sentiment: "Dear friends, I urge you, as aliens and strangers in the world" (1 Pet. 2:11). Our kingdom is not of this world. Yes, we live in it, but we are not of it. Jesus had to remind the Jews and His disciples that they cannot elevate themselves above the foreigner; in fact, they must love the foreigner as they love themselves.

That is the crux of the story of the Good Samaritan (see Luke 10:25-37). It was a Jew who was beaten up and left by the wayside. All the other Jews who saw this fellow in his poor condition passed him by. It was a foreigner who showed the law of love by caring for the man. And more, a foreigner had all the reason in the world to ignore this Jew whose people despised all others who were not racially Jewish. We might paraphrase the idea this way: "Love the foreigner like he loves you, then you will have obeyed all the commands of the Lord."

Jesus pushed the disciples on this point several times. The woman at the well would have been considered a half-breed in her day, yet Jesus makes sure the disciples get the point. Not only does He touch her with tender concern, He makes such an impact on her that she turns into an evangelist and brings the whole town to meet the prophet (see John 4:28-30). Again, the twist: a non-Jew showing people the way to God. Paul sums it up later with the statement, "There is neither Jew nor Greek" (Gal. 3:28).

That is our official Christian belief. Unfortunately, our lifestyle does not always match our beliefs.

The world today is desperate for the Christian message. Never before have there been so many different ethnic battles going on at the same time; thousands are being killed and millions are left destitute. The world does not know how to love the foreigner. It does not know how to accept others as equals. It does know how to hate. And it does so fiercely.

The Church needs to have a clear message of love and acceptance in this time of fission and fracture. We need to be the ones who model the message that we are all created with full and equal dignity. No one is to be pushed down for the purpose of elevating another. No one should presume himself to be more noble in race than another. It is true that the Church has lent its support to ethnic oppression, justifying the system of slavery, apartheid and condoning the mistreatment of Native Americans—just to name a few. We do need to be redeemed from that history.

Everything about it stands counter to the biblical mandates regarding love of the alien and stranger. We clearly cannot say we have loved them as we have loved ourselves.

The Church can take a fresh stand in this bitter and cruel hour. We believe the Holy Spirit will give us the power if we just take the step of faith.

63. Go for the Smorgasbord

Much of our church life in North America has been dominated by people who were more influenced by Madison Avenue than the Holy Spirit. We have been trained to maximize the size of our churches at the lowest possible cost. The message seems to be: Identify people who are just like yourselves and attract them into your church. The results would be a big congregation of people who look just like we do.

But that idea is not biblical. Israel was wrong to pursue a vision of religious life that looked just like them, and God condemned them for it. We need to learn from that history.

Although the Church Growth Movement has many good points, it can be taken too far. The Kingdom is not ruled by pragmatics, it is governed by values that reflect the heart of God. Our churches are to be models of that heart. Our corporate life together should demonstrate the integrity of a gospel that breaks down walls that divide. Our churches should send the clear message: Love is practiced here; not prejudice, racism and strife.

We believe that pastors and other leaders need to model institutions that physically demonstrate the gospel of Jesus Christ. Our churches cannot in good conscience look like a lunch bar that serves only white Wonder bread. We are the full-blown smorgasbord of God's creation, that place where all colors come together to celebrate in a spirit that stands in contrast to the world. We must proclaim by the life of our churches that the gospel is good news to *all* people and that it is a reconciling force for which the world desperately prays—no one wants the ethnic rape and ethnic cleansing that makes up much of the headlines today.

We recommend that you look for ways to move your church closer to a fully unified version of the Kingdom. Here are a few ways to start:

- Begin regular times of fellowship with pastors of other ethnic groups in your region. Pray, study and fellowship together. Do not make it all official—play in each other's homes, see movies together, attend community events.

- Think through ways you can share in each other's ministry and seek ways to learn from each other. Share the pulpits, have an occasional "swap" of Sunday School teachers, plan mutual events that involve the full participation of both churches.

- Begin to incorporate a broader ethnic form of worship in the regular service. Include different styles of music, stories of other cultures, performances by those from a tradition different from your own.

- As staff positions open up, make an aggressive search for ethnic diversity. Ask your ethnic pastors and friends to help you in this task.

- As your church begins to implement new programs, be careful to ask if they are in danger of reinforcing old patterns. Be creative and work hard to ensure you are thinking of the broader community. If you are ever stumped for ideas, call upon ethnic pastors.

64. Make Friends with International Students

People from around the world find the United States a good place to receive graduate and postgraduate education. Our campuses serve as an intersection of the nations. The opportunities for Christians to build bridges are tremendous. We have a few suggestions for how your church might do this:

- Join International Students, Inc. (ISI), a nonprofit ministry that helps Christians host internationals. If they have a chapter on your local college campus, become involved and ask them to help your church catch the vision.

- If an ISI chapter is not operating in your area, ask them to help organize one through your church. Take the lead in your area to launch a quality outreach to foreign students.

- Contact the local university and offer to help in international student orientation. They may be a little wary of your religious orientation, but if you present yourself as a help to their program—not an evangelistic outreach—they are sure to accept your participation. This will provide the opportunity to give practical assistance to foreign students as they adjust to this culture, and it will open the door for a deeper relationship for days ahead.

- Consider opening your home as a boarding option for international students. Universities

are often looking for these leads, because they
have discovered that students adjust much
more easily with that kind of specific attention.
Several members in your church might like to
open their homes in this way.

- Attend cultural events on the campus. This will
  give you an appreciation for other cultures
  and, again, open the door for relationships.

65. Provide Tutoring

Los Angeles is the immigration capital of America. It is the
world's second largest Guatemalan, Mexican, Salvadoran,
Filipino and Korean city. It is an official sanctuary to immigrants, providing protection against certain federal laws. It
grows by at least 500,000 foreigners a year (more than the
entire population of Wyoming) and has schools that look
like mini United Nations centers—some have students
speaking in as many as 35 languages.

These broad demographics create certain challenges.
Dozens of Christian ministries and churches have noticed
the need to help young kids make it through the early years
of school. When 140 first-generation ethnic groups converge
in the city, a good number of kids come from homes where
parents cannot help with schoolwork. They simply do not
understand the language. Even though these kids regress in
their work, most are simply passed through the system and
graduated. They have minimal language and arithmetic skills,
and they perpetuate the problems of being an immigrant.

Some churches have established first-rate tutoring programs for these youths. They stay close to both the families
and the teachers to ensure the progress is sound. The volunteers who tutor are, in most cases, teachers themselves, so
they bring the experience and skill to do a good job.

Another form of tutoring that works well in Los Angeles is adult literacy instruction and job skills training. People are given the tools to make it for themselves in the big city. Rather than facing unemployment, welfare, homelessness and a potential life of crime, they are helped by Christians to become productive, happy members of the city. And this has benefits for the church members involved, too, as they also get the privilege of attending to people's spiritual needs.

We think these churches and ministries are 100 percent on the mark with what it means to serve the alien. We highly recommend you follow their model if you have foreigners living in your area.

66. Advocate for Immigrants

Perhaps one of the reasons the Bible places such a strong emphasis on caring for the alien is that they are extremely vulnerable to unfair practices. To advocate for them is to represent their case, to speak up for them and ask for justice and mercy. In our travels, we have met a great number of pastors who are successfully advocating on behalf of foreigners. Here are a few ideas should you decide to lead your church in speaking out in this way:

- Establish a basic legal service. Several churches have lawyers who provide a "quick scan" service of all rental, employment and purchase agreements for those who have just moved from another country. The lawyers ensure that these people are not being cheated. If you offer a service like this, you won't have to do much promotion; word travels fast in the immigrant community.

- Help with landlord problems. This has to be the most common abuse situation. Toilets don't flush, baths don't drain, windows are shattered, doors don't lock, the gas stove leaks. Unfortunately, some landlords apparently just don't care about the safety, health and rights of immigrants. We have found that churches and their partnering law firms are able to extract fast service with a letter to a landlord that lists the grievances of the tenant "client." This also works well with unjust evictions.

- The other area in which advocacy has been helpful is protecting these aliens from crooked dentists and doctors. Ailments continue to emerge and bills continue to appear in a manner that could never happen to a fully fluent resident. Letters from the law firm or church office interrupt these practices fairly rapidly.

67. Go to the Immigrant

You may live in the inner city or a neighborhood that is well stocked with foreigners. If so, you are acquainted with their world.

But perhaps you live in the suburbs or a rural area where everyone is pretty much like you. If that is the case, this idea is for you. We suggest that you find ways to learn about immigrants through hands-on exposure. Here are a few ways to go about this:

- Look up the international ethnic pastors in town. Tell them you are interested in learning more about their culture and specific challenges. Be aware that many cultures are much more quiet and self-effacing than our own. It

will take time to establish the kind of relationship where they will feel free to share some of
the more difficult aspects of their lives.

- Attend the international cultural events in your
  town. Your local newspaper probably lists such
  activities, or you can call the appropriate city
  administration office.

- Arrange for weekend plunges for you and
  some church members where you spend a couple of nights and days in the homes of foreigners. You can set up your contacts through the
  pastors you have met. If this goes well, consider a summer excursion for some of the church's
  youth. They will bring back their invaluable
  experience right into the heart of the church.

68. Give to the Immigrant

Our suggestion here is very direct—nonprofit ministries
that help the church orient itself to the foreigner do not
receive much assistance. We hope that you will consider
motivating your church to make a sizeable donation to the
work of International Students, Inc. (they are listed in the
resource section). Their visionary work deserves the enthusiastic partnership of the Church.

We also recommend that you consider supporting international refugees. Today, close to 20 million people have
had to flee from their homes due to war, famine and drought
(sadly, more than 95 percent of them because of war). They
face additional danger because of potential encounters with
unruly soldiers, and they certainly face the ominous cloud
of death through starvation, dehydration and disease. Several
international relief and development agencies are concerned

about these refugees. They provide expert help, and they bring a Christian ethic to the entire process.

69. Spread the Vision for Befriending Immigrants

Choose a day on your annual church calendar to highlight the call to care for foreigners. Here are some ideas you might implement:

- Prepare that Sunday's service around the call to care for foreigners. Remember, shortly after Jesus was born, He and His parents fled as alien refugees.

- Ask all the Sunday School teachers to incorporate the theme of caring for immigrants into that week's lesson.

- During the church service, present current statistics on the global situation. Offer practical suggestions on how Christians can make a difference.

- Invite local international students to come and share some of their experiences since moving to this country. Ask them to tell the church something about their home country.

- If you have made friends with local immigrant pastors, ask them to participate in the service. As an expression of our bond of love and unity in the family of faith, ask them to help lead the entire congregation in communion.

- If any of your members have international guests living in their homes, let these guests take part in the service.

- Collect a special offering for ISI or a relief agency that works with refugees.

- Offer a Saturday or Sunday afternoon seminar for those who would like to learn more about this type of ministry. Perhaps you could build a "plunge" experience into the day.

70. Resources for Helping Immigrants

ORGANIZATIONS

INTERNATIONAL STUDENTS, INC.
P.O. Box C
Colorado Springs, CO 80901
We think this is the key organization to help you focus on international students. They publish an excellent curriculum guide entitled *How to Develop an International Student Ministry: A Church Ministry Manual.* They also publish a series of booklets on becoming friends with people of other cultures.

LITERACY VOLUNTEERS OF AMERICA
5795 Widewaters Parkway
Syracuse, NY 13214
Contact this group for help with teaching literacy to foreigners who require the assistance.

WORLD CONCERN
19303 Fremont Avenue North
Seattle, WA 99111
This group will channel your money to refugees.

WORLD RELIEF
P.O. Box WRC
Wheaton, IL 60189
This group will help you steer your funds
to the refugee.

WORLD VISION
919 W. Huntington Dr.
Monrovia, CA 91016
This is the world's largest Christian relief
and development organization.

BOOKS
More Than Equals by Chris Rice and
Spencer Perkins (InterVarsity, 1993).
*The Friendship Gap: Reaching Out Across
Cultures* by Tim Stafford (InterVarsity,
1984).
The World at Your Doorstep by Lawson Lau
(InterVarsity, 1984).

X.
THE FAMILY
Affirming the Institution Ordained by God

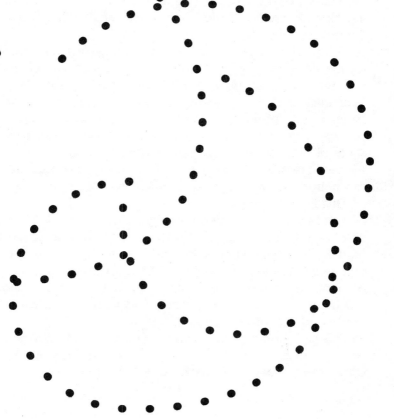

It seems America has lost its home. This tragedy is measured at several points: The majority of today's kids come from divided families—either living with a single parent or a stepparent; most children and teens come home to an empty house after school—the so-called "latchkey kids"; no one knows the exact statistics, but we hear that as many as 1 in 5 kids will be sexually or physically molested in their homes by a family member; and for some 20 million American kids, home does not provide the kinds of protection, warm beds and full meals that make up part of the romantic picture of the family—because they live below the poverty line.

If you ask today's college students about their prospects for marriage and a good family life, more than 70 percent will tell you flat out that the concept does not work. Celebrities on the talk show circuit refer to their former marriages as one of those "growing-up phases" that is important in the maturation years but irrelevant in the more adult stage of life. The idea of one relationship enduring over *many* phases of life is impractical and even boring. Kids can neither demand nor expect a two-parent upbringing.

This is not a pretty picture.

The bleak outlook on the family is not confined to secular society either. Research shows that Christian youths hold the same dim view of family-in-the-future as their secular peers. Somehow the preaching and teaching of our pastors and bigger-than-life ministry leaders has not turned our hearts toward home. Instead, our hearts are sick with doubt and despair.

This fact should shake us and force us to examine where we have missed the mark. Why do our own kids see our Christian marriages and say no to the future?

We think the Church has let society down by failing to ensure the strength of the family. Rather than affirm the God-designed family structure, we have followed society's lead by allowing our commitments to wane.

Through our disregard for the family, we have failed to serve as salt and light to our society. The single greatest tragedy for the Church and our society in the 1980s was the new pattern of systematic separation from the world. We taught from the pulpit, radio and TV that Christians should fear the world, build fortress walls around our homes and schools, and hide our kids from the ravages of society. Rather than love the world, we despised and rejected it. In fact, from a biblical point of view, we robbed the world. We stole from them the gift of the Holy Spirit—the fragrance of our lives.

Private schools, private clubs for kids, private parties, private lives. Jesus' question has more relevance to us today than perhaps any other time in the history of the Church: "If the salt loses its saltiness, how can it be made salty again? It is no longer good for anything, except to be thrown out and trampled by men" (Matt. 5:13).

The Church family needs to return to the world. Any other choice is immoral.

71. Move Beyond the Law

We believe we fail our kids and the world by preaching a rigid, imbalanced structure for the family. Certain churches have urged their men to "take over" and rule with sole authority, ignoring the biblical role of their wives. They maintain that "lead the family" means having authoritative rule of the roost, albeit in a "loving" way. Although many women *are* called by God to stay at home (an honorable occupation), others are told they must stay at home. Those who teach this thinking, it seems, believe more in the law of control than in the law of love.

However, God never intended for women to give up their responsibility to be disciples of—and for—Christ. They do not have the privilege to follow Christ through their husbands—they must follow Him as copartners *with* their husbands. A curious thing happens to many Christian marriages between the altar and the hearth: women who at one moment were intelligent, self-directed and aflame in their passion to serve Christ suddenly lose the ability to take charge of themselves and they turn their passions solely toward their husbands. God meant for women to grow and flourish in their personal lives and service to Him. If the Church does not affirm and champion the role of women, it will suffer a great loss in its effort to reach the world.

Just as we have learned that the Church's earlier justification of racism was not biblical, we must also learn that sexism cannot be biblically supported. As the world confers equal status on women, they will watch to see how the Church responds. Will we cling to rigid, outdated roles or will we offer our full, enthusiastic support of women? We must choose to fight for women's status as full partners of God. If not, we may watch our own daughters say "no thanks" to our hallowed rules and hollow religion.

A large number of people within the Church today love Jesus dearly and are thankful for the forgiveness of their sins; they witness to their neighbors and raise wonderful God-loving families. These men and women take their Bibles so seriously that they cannot accept sexism in the Church as an interpretation of the Word.

Still, we think that not enough men have given an honest look at the Bible's view of women. Our energy has not been applied to the more serious question of our day. We have listed some helpful books and organizations in the resource section for those who would like to venture deeper into this issue.

72. Soften the Blows for Stressed-out Families

We know it from all the counseling and prayer sessions in our churches: For many people, managing family life is nothing more than a full-time job of survival. The kids' homework is never complete; house projects are half done; sports activities are only occasionally attended; the house is not quite clean enough; bills are not paid on time. Those overwhelmed by the demands of family life feel like they are only treading water—eventually their legs will tire out and they will slowly sink.

Our suggestion is that churches look out for families in this situation. Most often, those with the biggest struggles are single moms with young children. Be practical in your help in the same way a doctor would be practical with a patient bleeding in the emergency room. Here are a few ideas:

- Establish a car repair service for people who are suffering the transportation blues. Broken-down vehicles can cause a lot of problems: work is missed, income is lost, the schedule must be juggled, kids may be late to school. Mechanics can make a good sum of money off the uninformed motorist. Offering the services of a trustworthy mechanic from your congregation can be a great blessing to someone in need. Often a simple tune-up, adjustment or inexpensive new part can restore a car to full use.

- Watch for sickness in these overworked families. You may have health specialists in your church who could offer advice to keep the body and mind well during prolonged times of stress.

- Offer a no-holds-barred workshop on dealing

with financial troubles. Some people simply need basic instruction in money management to get them on track; others may need a frank discussion on poor spending habits. One church discovered that several of its members dealt with depression over financial problems by going on shopping sprees with their credit cards. The best thing that ever happened to these folks was the creation of a "no credit card" support group.

- Strive to create a church environment where people naturally look out for members who seem to be struggling. Timely words of encouragement and specific offers of help feel like a cold glass of water amidst the drought.

73. Provide a Positive Sexual Orientation for Youth

You only need to flip the TV channels or browse at the magazine rack to realize that teenagers are being misled when it comes to sexuality. And they won't have a chance to develop a clear, biblical ethic of sexuality unless the Church offers a strong and friendly alternative to the cultural norm. We suggest several action steps:

- We need to teach a positive attitude toward sexuality. In reaction to the flagrant sexuality of society, we have turned negative, appearing uncomfortable with how God created us. We were made sexual. We are passionate, desiring intimacy both physically and emotionally. That is part of God's idea. He created sex. Our youth need to hear about the enjoyment of sexuality—not just that it is "bad." We must tell them that sex is terrific, in its proper place. We can promote the idea that the best sex happens in the context of marriage. Young people will be much more likely to hear our message to "wait" if they know the prevailing cultural norm is not the only pleasurable road.

- We need to give youth straightforward information and frank advice about sexuality. It is not fair for churches to withdraw from education about how the body works. We live in a society so full of invitation and intrigue that it seems normal for youth to become sexually active. Open, direct discussions about sex, birth control, pregnancy and disease is owed to them. We need to be careful to distinguish our moralizing from the facts. If not, they will be suspect of our motives and likely to reject our advice, confusing it as "mom's and dad's opinion."

- Sponsor youth seminars on sexuality. Excellent materials (listed in the resource section) and speakers are available to help you put together a meaningful program.

74. Create a Pregnancy Center

Your church could provide an invaluable service to women who are pregnant. Throughout the United States, church leaders have been recognizing that caring for someone who is with child is a form of ministry that reaches deep into that person's soul.

Several churches are establishing pregnancy centers, either on the church premises using their own volunteer staff, or through a consortium of local churches. Operating the center can be a task of several proportions: Some churches operate them a couple days each week, some every morning (including Saturdays for those who work), and others manage to maintain a full-time center.

The key to these centers is a friendly atmosphere, offering services that help women deal with the various stages and consequences of pregnancy. The goal is never to "entrap" women to lead them to Jesus or fill their minds with "right" thinking. The goal is to provide true service. The opportunities to assist women in their discipleship with Christ will flow naturally from the genuine love and care. Here are some of the services you or a group of churches could offer:

- Free pregnancy tests.

- Prenatal counseling on health care and stress management.

- Practical assistance in finding a job or new housing when needed.

- Connecting the women to good physicians.

- Counseling for their partners, if possible.

- Referral service for women who may be considering adopting out the child, and the full support of the staff through that noble and difficult choice.

- Linking women to Nurturing Network, an organization that helps women relocate during the pregnancy if bearing the child has strong, negative social implications.

- Providing baby clothes and equipment for the first few months of infancy.

- Providing meals and transportation during the first few months of postpartum recovery.

75. Go with the Family

Churches need to think through inexpensive and uncomplicated means for the family to spend quality time together. We recommend that you create a small committee of energetic parents for the sole purpose of designing family events.

These activities need to reinforce the family unit (everyone should leave thinking that it was great to be together) and they should not be "teaching" events that underline how badly we have messed up! Also, make sure these do not become another form of the Church withdrawing from society. If you are creative enough to think up fun ideas, you will be able to attract your own peers and your children's peers to join the events. Here are a few possible activities to get you thinking:

- Go to local museums and art exhibits.

- When the weather is good, sponsor regular barbecues complete with games and sports activities. Choose a convenient location, such as the city park.

- Plan an annual weekend camp-out that is affordable and not a hassle to get to. Have someone in charge of camping equipment for people who do not have the goods.

- Attend family-oriented plays sponsored by the local university or community theater group.

- Have get-togethers or parties on holidays

and other special occasions. In one small town, a group of churches gets together to host an annual Halloween blowout. One church gymnasium holds dozens of game booths, and a best-costume contest. The event now draws almost all of the parents and children from the participating churches. Besides providing fun and recreation, it is also a great model of how churches can work together for the common good.

76. Give to the Family

Here are three ways we suggest your church give financially to help the family. First, we think you should focus on local needs. Perhaps you could create a benevolent fund that is administered without much red tape. This could be overseen by someone on location who can discern quickly what kinds of donations could help a family in need. That might be in the form of cash, a gift certificate for the local grocery store or canned goods that are kept in a church pantry. The fund could be a simple formula—for example, one percent of every Sunday's offering. This could be set up in a separate checking account.

Second, also on the local level, help fund a pregnancy center, as we described earlier. If your town does not already have such a center, perhaps you could join a few local pastors and create a budget for one that operates on donated labor.

Third, we urge you to consider the ongoing work of international relief and development ministries. They perform a wonderful service to families caught in poverty around the world. We mentioned World Vision and World Relief in Section II of this book; your money will be carefully and wisely spent by them.

77. Spread the Vision for Strong Families

Choose a Sunday on your annual church calendar to emphasize the biblical call to care for the family. Here are a few suggestions for that day:

- Plan the Sunday service around the theme of the family. Don't go for the old standby about how wives should submit to their husbands and children should honor their father and mother, and all that. Think of the wonderful accounts of how God used the family in Bible days.

- Ask your Sunday School teachers to have the subject of family central to that week's lesson.

- Invite local ministries working with the family to talk about their work. You may ask the county department of family services to come and describe typical family issues in your area.

- Pray together for God's grace and intervention to keep families strong.

- Plan a Saturday or Sunday afternoon seminar for those members who would like to become more involved in family concerns.

- If you have a local pregnancy center, see if you can take an "offering" of volunteer hours—people who would be willing to help out at the center.

- If you have single parents in the church, provide a forum to share the triumphs and

the tragedies of that lifestyle. It is always
good to have our sensitivities increased.

78. Resources for the Family

Several family-oriented organizations and publishers are
already familiar to the evangelical world. We have chosen
to highlight some other resources that may not be as well
known.

ORGANIZATIONS

CHRISTIANS FOR BIBLICAL EQUALITY
380 Lafayette Road, South
Suite 122
St. Paul, MN 55107

JOSH McDOWELL MINISTRIES
P.O. Box 1000
Dallas, TX 75221
This group provides good resources for
youth and sexuality issues.

NURTURING NETWORK
P.O. Box 2050
Boise, ID 83701

BOOKS

Equal to Serve by Gretchen Gaebelien Hull
(Revell, 1987).
Paul, Women and Wives by Craig Keener
(Hendrickson, 1992).
*Recovering Biblical Manhood and
Womanhood* by John Piper and Wayne
Grudem (Crossway, 1991).
Shame-Free Parenting by Sandra Wilson
(InterVarsity, 1992).

When Child Abuse Comes to the Church by
Bill Anderson, (Bethany House, 1992).

MAGAZINES

Priscilla Papers
380 Lafayette Road, South
Suite 122
St. Paul, MN 55107

Urban Family
P.O. Box 40125
Pasadena, CA 91104

XI.
THE OPPRESSED
Upholding the Downtrodden

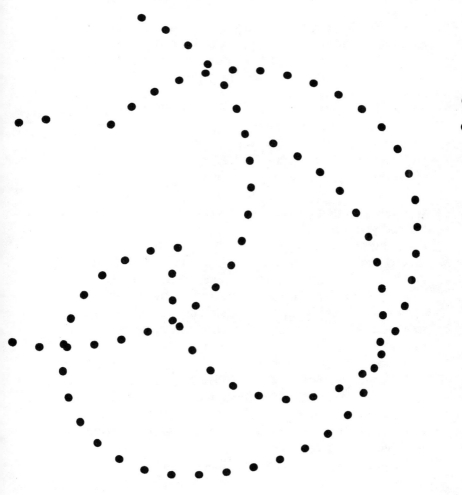

Earlier, we spoke of Christianity having its roots in the sense of being "foreigners"—strangers in a strange land.

We also have a sense of oppression in our roots. Much of Israel's literature seems to recall the days of exile in Egypt. The feeling is that God showered extreme favor on the nation by freeing them from the tyrannical rule of Pharaoh. And at times when Israel seemed to forget the name of the Lord and drifted from His ordinances, Yahweh reminded them of the days of exile. He says, "Don't you remember when I brought you up out of the land of Egypt?" (see Num. 24:8 and Deut. 6:21,22).

God instructed Israel regularly on the need to help those who were oppressed. The implication was that their future well-being depended on their obedience to this command. "Would you like your light to shine?" asks the prophet, "Then do away with oppression" (see Isa. 58; Amos 8:4-10). In a time of frustration when the Lord did not seem to hear the cry of Israel, another prophet asks, "What does the Lord require of you?" It is to "act justly and to love mercy and to walk humbly with your God" (Micah 6:8). Israel understood that God was not entertained by the structure and patterns of worship if it did not lead to doing justice.

In the New Testament, Jesus continues the conversation with Israel's religious leaders. In His famous "Woe to you" speech (see Matt. 23), He chides them for being extremely zealous in their religion but missing the substance of their calling. In fact, they are so far off the mark that their missionary work produces converts who are "twice the sons of hell as you are" (see v. 15). Jesus tells them they have put their focus on issues such as tithing and keeping the Sabbath while neglecting "the more important matters of the law—justice, mercy and faithfulness" (v. 23). It is here that Jesus tells them they have been so careful in their filtering of the law that they have managed to strain out a gnat but swallow a came (see v. 24).

These are not flattering words. Of course, Jesus had the authority to say them.

We wonder what His words would be to us today. How have we "done justice" and attended to the needs of the oppressed? Doing justice is a demanding ministry. It requires us to go beyond the routines of church attendance, prayer meetings and offerings. It also requires us to go beyond the ministry of meeting people's immediate needs—such as hunger or shelter. Justice asks us to look at the systems that cause people's pain; to go beneath the surface of pain and change the way the world works.

We think it is unfortunate that the Church has not led the way in our nation for justice. We do not have the reputation for defending the rights of those who are oppressed. In fact, we have, historically, tended to side with those who were doing the oppressing, casting shadows of doubt on people who cry foul. In some cases, the Church has had a strange double standard.

When the Soviet Union used to be a country, churches were vocal about the abuses of power going on there. We rightly understood that the government was being unjust and needed to be called to account for unfair treatment of innocent citizens. But we were never able to turn the spotlight around on our own country and question our historical abuse of ethnic groups, nor contemporary cases of abuse. We largely "shrugged off" our own national policies that supported the evil governments, such as El Salvador, where thousands of civilians were being killed through systematic torture.

Unfortunately, more than anything else, we lost our integrity. Our motives were suspect when we were always able to see the speck in the other country's eyes but never acknowledge the log in our own.

It happens in this country as well. At a recent march of gays in downtown Philadelphia, scores of Christians showed up to shout slogans of condemnation at the men and women who were quietly making the case that they should have equal rights. Through the din of shouts, a soft chorus of voices began to grow: "Jesus loves me this I know." The gays were singing about someone who died as an outcast—someone with whom they felt some solidarity. The Christians' response was to increase the volume of their derisive slogans.

Whatever you believe about the gay rights movement, we think you would agree that chanting slogans that put down gays is not the way to win them over or show them Christ's love. Some would argue that such a cold response is not true of all of us. Perhaps, but we cannot say the Church has led our society in the way of compassion.

As church leaders, we have the opportunity in the days ahead to clean the slate, to stand for justice, to counter the prevailing sense that our God condones oppression. We need to feel a strong jealousy for the name of Jesus and get the public record straight. Jesus is not only opposed to oppression, He Himself died an unjust death through a flimflam trial in Jerusalem. Jesus is a friend to the oppressed, and as such, we must work diligently to "act justly and to love mercy and to walk humbly with our God."

79. Go Public

The public is used to knee-jerk responses from some Christian leaders on certain issues. We may think we are standing up for righteousness, but in the world's eyes, we are often whining—complaining that society is not being fair to the Church.

We think that leaders should surprise the public with a quiet yet persistent campaign of making our opinions known to the public regarding the treatment of *others*—people who may or may not follow the Lord but who are being oppressed by certain laws or ordinances that are not fair.

We recommend you write letters to the editor of the local newspaper and national magazines. Sign it with your title and religious affiliation. Some editors may print your letter just out of intrigue that your voice seems to be contrary to typical religious opinion. The president of a missionary society to Muslims wrote a long letter to the editor of the *Los Angeles Times* lambasting the federal government's unfair treatment of Muslim Palestinians. The letter said that these men and women were not given due process during a trial. No one would have expected an organization that works to "convert" Muslims to defend them. The director of the organization received many notes of thanks and admiration.

If college students attend your church, encourage them to write letters to the editor of their campus newspaper. They, too, are used to receiving reactionary mail from Christians—not pieces that defend the rights of the oppressed. These students' letters are sure to get published.

80. Tame the Tongue

Racism and sexism are often passed on unconsciously through our language. When we begin to tolerate these subtle slurs, the belief creeps in that certain kinds of people are not as equal as others. Oppression always happens in the context of one group belittling another. You cannot oppress someone who you feel is your peer in every good sense of that word.

In Isaiah 58, God tells Israel that malicious talk is on the same level as oppression. The apostle James tells us that an untamed tongue can cause a forest fire, destroying everything in its path (see Jas. 3:1-12). Some enlightening studies have been done on the language used regarding Jews during the late 1800s and early 1900s. Few opposed the incredibly ugly and vicious terms used to describe Jews. And Christians were almost entirely silent. By the time a program of annihilation was implemented by Hitler, many people had been indoctrinated with the belief that Jews were a little below everyone else.

Pastors need to take the lead in helping both the Church and society speak well of others. We should feel uncomfortable about jokes and labels that categorize others in ways that dehumanize them. It is Christian to always speak the truth and to proclaim the dignity of all people. Some particular areas of concern include:

- Language about women. Christians seem to be the last people getting on board with this one. We are comfortable to think of men as "men" and women as "gals." Some teachers subtly convey that certain jobs only a man can do and certain things a woman just cannot understand. Men need to be completely at peace with themselves, but that does not give them permission to belittle women, just as being white does not give us permission to belittle blacks, or vice versa.

- Language about internationals, especially Arabs, Muslims, Japanese and Mexicans. Few endearing terms are used for these people but plenty of hurtful images exist. It does no good to perpetuate misguided stereotypes.

- Language against gays. It does not matter how much we may oppose someone's lifestyle, that does not permit us to belittle them. If we truly believe their practices are harmful and wrong, then we should try to win them over with love, respect and understanding. We should always be on the lookout for ways to build bridges, not widen the chasm by using offensive terms and language.

81. Learn About Others' Heritage

One of the greatest ways to compliment someone is to try to learn from them. More than that, however, it has a certain equalizing power—I need you, you need me. This exchange can also lead to a healthy admiration of the other person's culture and background.

Most people are not aware, for example, that several important medical discoveries, mathematical systems and Western architectural styles came from the Arab culture. We are indebted to them for their genius and creative eye. But these facts have been hidden from us, not by some cynical design but by stereotypes about them and the subtle mistrust we have been taught.

We suggest you make a commitment to learn the heritage of a group of people who have been oppressed in the past and perhaps are still being oppressed today. If possible, learn about a group of people in your region. This makes the new information more poignant and personal. These are some of the ways you could go about this:

- Ask your local librarian for help in researching the idea.

- If you live near a university, you have a wealth of resources available through the ethnic centers. They will provide you with material that records history from a different orientation. This is a benefit,

because we have usually only been
taught our own version.

- Attend cultural events that teach more
  about the people you are studying.

- Enjoy the artistic side of their culture—
  view their art, listen to their music,
  read their stories and poetry.

- Experience their cuisine.

You may discover that your church high school group
would be interested in this process. They could help assemble material for class credit, go on field trips or spend an
evening listening to music. If you have a college group,
see if you could recruit a couple of students to help study
a different people group.

82. Go to the Oppressed

We have one suggestion for you here. Arrange a field trip
or short-term mission trip to visit people who have historically been oppressed. You can go about this in a variety
of ways. If you live near a Native American Reserve, contact the appropriate officials and explain that your church
knows little about their customs, traditions and beliefs.
Assure them you have no missionary intentions; your desire
is to learn. In most cases, you will find people happy to
cooperate and explain history from their orientation.

You may want to venture out a little further, perhaps to
Central America or the Caribbean. If so, contact BridgeBuilders
(see "resources" in section IV) for help with designing a trip.

If you are part of a denomination, contact the headquarters to learn of any work they have done to orient members to oppressed groups. They may have a field trip program that would meet your needs. Several universities offer study trips in the summer. These are usually hosted by Native Americans and last a couple of days. They are introductory and serve as a great way to begin the learning process.

83. Give to the Oppressed

Most churches have some kind of library. If your church has a fairly large one, or if another part of the church could function as a display area, establish a learning center about a group of people that has been historically oppressed.

By giving to them, we are suggesting you establish a creative display that serves to document their history and culture. This establishes them as real to your congregation. You have given them real names and faces, and you have provided some recognition and respect. If your church is blessed with artistic people, this could become a fairly ambitious project as you collect artifacts, pictures, textiles, stories and books. You may want to seek help from your local university. This display could grow as you add a little more each year. Make it a friendly setup to enable members to sit down and read a book, thumb through some stories and study the art.

Another approach could be to bring together several local pastors around the idea. Go to your local library as a team and ask if they would be interested in a cooperative effort to establish a display in the library to benefit the entire community. This group approach could result in the volunteer help of several prominent community members and the financial backing of local business leaders. And you would be sure to garner the interest of the local newspaper.

We think it makes good sense for the Church to provide this kind of leadership. It is biblical to show our dignity and respect for all of God's people, and it is smart to keep high the public admiration for Christian values.

84. Spread the Vision for Upholding the Downtrodden

Choose a Sunday on your annual church calendar to focus on the Bible's call to care for the oppressed. Here are some of the elements you could build into that day:

- Have the church service feature the subject of oppressed people and the Christian's duty to uphold them.

- Ask the Sunday School teachers to incorporate the theme of the oppressed into that week's lesson.

- Ask a local member of a traditionally oppressed group to come and share some of their history and culture with the congregation.

- Spend a focused time of prayer asking God to cleanse the Church of its own racism, sexism and pride. Ask for wisdom to live justly in your relationships with other people.

- Create a bulletin insert that suggests appropriate language for how we refer to others. Highlight the offensive language that we would want to eliminate from our speech.

- Offer a Saturday or Sunday afternoon seminar for those who would like to explore the idea of biblical justice further.

- This would be a good Sunday to take sign-ups for a field trip or short-term mission trip to a historically oppressed group.

85. Resources for Helping the Oppressed

ORGANIZATIONS

AMNESTY INTERNATIONAL
322 Eighth Ave.
New York, NY 10001

ASSOCIATION FOR PUBLIC JUSTICE
321 8th Street, NE
Washington, D.C. 20002

BOOKS

Agenda for Biblical People by
Jim Wallis (HarperCollins, 1984).
Equal to Serve by Gretchen Gaebelien Hull
(Revell, 1987).
Let Justice Roll Down by John Perkins
(Regal, 1976).
Liberating News by Orlando Costas
(Eerdmans, 1989).
With Justice for All by John Perkins
(Regal, 1982).
The above Regal books by John Perkins
are available from: John Perkins Foundation
1581 Navarro
Pasadena, CA 91103

MAGAZINES

Religion and Democracy Report
1331 H. Street NW, Suite 900
Washington, DC 20005

Sojourners
P.O. Box 29272
Washington, DC 20017

XII.
THE DISABLED
Regaining the Dignity of Disability

The name "Israel" signifies so much to the Christian Church. It is our roots, our heritage, our compass. It was God who chose the name Israel, and He conferred the name to Jacob after spending the night wrestling with him in a tent. It happened that Jacob would not let go of God until He promised to bless him and his offspring. God apparently let the fight continue to measure Jacob's determination to know the blessing of Yahweh's hand.

By sunrise, it was clear. And as a mark of God's approval, He put Jacob's hip out of joint. Then He changed Jacob's name to "Israel," and all of Christianity draws its heritage from that night of struggle. Israel, the man, would limp for the rest of his life. (See Genesis 32:22-32.) The blessing and the hardship; the presence and the pain; the heavens and the earth. The nation of Israel would live out the same tension in its days of searching Yahweh's hand of blessing. Their struggle continues.

We missed the importance of Israel in our life. Perhaps we should commission paintings for the vestibules of our churches to remind us of the heritage of Israel. In a mystical way, physical disability points us to the Creator and breathes the prayer, "Don't let me go!" It reminds us of the struggle of life and calls us to worship the One who creates it.

We need to regain the dignity of disability. We need to attach ourselves to the integrity it offers our discipleship. We need to depend on its power to pray our deepest thoughts and lead us through the tunnels of our heart's great questions.

"My God, my God, why have you forsaken me?" (Ps. 22:1).
"I will never leave you nor forsake you" (Heb. 13:5, NKJV).

The Old Testament offers a picture of the day when the lame will throw aside their crutches and run at full pace to the city of Zion (see Isa. 35). There will be great laughter and tears of joy, for in that day we shall all be made fully whole—body, soul and spirit. The night of struggle and the lifetime of limping will be over. The redemption will be final and complete. The story belongs to all of us.

We are wrong to push aside those with physical disabilities, to relegate them to a lesser place in the order of life and church. Indeed, it may be more appropriate to assign people with physical disabilities a place of honor in this life—slightly higher than the rest of us. They more perfectly reflect Israel's night of struggle; they more honestly exhibit the truth regarding the human condition. It is through them that we are taught we cannot have Christ without the cross. We are dishonest to imply that the spirit and the body are so easily disjoined. No, we all wait for that great day of redemption because we all limp, in some way, through our years.

86. Bridge the Gulf

Many people feel uncomfortable around those with disabilities. Our quest for immortality, our culture's fixation with the "perfect" body and high society's club of the "beautiful people" are all barriers to the gospel fact that God created us all in love and dignity. We all carry the full measure of His image in us. The Church needs to stand against the lie that handicapped people are lesser beings and begin to reflect the truth of God's creation.

Our suggestion is simple enough. We think that church leaders need to call their local churches to bridge the gulf that separates people in our society according to physical capabilities. Begin to model through your church the kind of community that bears the marks of the Kingdom. Here are a few ideas:

- Make sure the church is suitable for people who
  have physical limitations. Build ramps, special
  seating areas and rest rooms that are accessible.

- Get the word out that you want to bring the
  disabled into the regular life of the church
  because you need them. Ask for volunteers to
  provide regular transportation and other services for those who require assistance.

- Think through the Sunday routine. How can
  you better incorporate handicapped people
  into the church service? Perhaps a part of the
  service could be regularly led by people with
  physical disabilities.

87. Provide Trauma Support

Disabilities often occur through a sudden accident or an
unexplained disease that shuts down part of the body. Tasks
that were once routine become extremely difficult or impossible. And legion issues and concerns loom: What about the
job? Who will pay the bills? Who will play with the kids? Will
people accept me? What about my spouse's view of me?

You may have people in your church who have suffered
the excruciating transition from being mobile and agile to
disabled. Here are a few steps you could take to help them
in this time of need:

- Try to meet with several people who have suffered severe, disabling accidents. Ask them to
  describe the emotions they experienced as a
  result of their misfortune. How have they
  moved beyond that point? What advice can
  they give you about reaching out to people in
  this situation?

- Ask members of your congregation to
  consider forming a special support
  group for people who have just acquired
  a severe disability. Make sure the team is
  diverse in its representation of experience
  with physical pain. Ask them to search out
  the people in need and focus their care
  upon them.

88. Help Find Jobs for the Disabled

If your church is typical, you will have several members who own businesses. Hopefully, they have accepted a "Kingdom perspective" of their companies and want to use them for God's glory. It may be possible for these entrepreneurs to employ some of the handicapped people in your church.

We are not proposing that companies create charity positions for the disabled. That would be demeaning. We do, however, propose that you encourage business owners to look for specific slots that could be filled by people who have physical disabilities. Any time it is possible, these slots should be reserved for disabled people, because they have a tough enough time finding work as it is. We are sure that Christian-led companies should be taking the lead in this area. Wouldn't it be great if the business community and the news media rushed to try and figure out why these businesses insist on such a practice and still make a good profit?

We suggest one other idea. Get your key businesspersons and disabled people together in one room at the church for a meeting. Open with the question: Do you suppose it is possible for all of us in this room to create a brand-new business together that would provide a valuable service to our community, employ an unusually large percentage of disabled people and turn a good profit? The outcome might surprise everyone.

89. Go with the Disabled

One of our fondest memories is of racing through the slums of Mexico City with Tom Brewster. A quadriplegic due to a swimming accident, Tom put most of us to shame with his energy and vision for life. He and his wife, Betty Sue, founded a revolutionary school of language learning that is relationally based versus academic. Tom insisted that language is not a barrier to overcome but a gift that can link us to people of other cultures. He modeled his theory.

It was not easy to keep up with Tom in the slums as he negotiated ruts and rocks in the outlying districts of Mexico City. He was there to teach us how to build relationships with people across cultures, and we have not forgotten his remarkable ability to make friends with all sorts of people. Tom is with Jesus now. His body finally gave in to the deterioration caused by organ failure. He is probably still arguing with Jesus for taking him home too soon. He had much to explore yet and all kinds of people to meet.

Our suggestion is based on our loving memory of Tom: Be sure to include people with disabilities in your short-term mission projects. Involve them in the planning process, both for their unique ministry ideas and their understanding of how to accommodate certain disabilities. Your trip will be all the richer, and your team will look a little more like the Kingdom.

90. Give to the Disabled

It is appropriate to ask what services we can provide for the disabled. Certain tasks in life require mechanical skills and strength that may be beyond the scope of people with disabilities.

Call a meeting with the disabled members in your congregation, and ask, "How can we help you? Are there certain tasks members of our church could perform to help you?" Write the list on a chalkboard and then brainstorm together a system that is both dignified and practical. We know of a church that recruited several members to be available to help disabled members. When these needs were called in to the church, they were simply forwarded to the volunteers.

However you go about this, keep in mind that it always needs to occur in the spirit of equality and dignity. All of us depend on others—the mechanic, doctor, teacher, counselor—for certain needs. We are simply extending the notion into the Body. And we encourage churches not to confine these services to the members of their congregation. Our mandate calls us to always look outside our own circle. Seek out people beyond your church who could use help.

91. Spread the Vision for Dignifying Disability

Choose a day on your annual church calendar to emphasize God's love for the disabled. Here are a few ideas:

- Plan the Sunday service around the theme of disability.

- Ask your Sunday School teachers to do the same for that week's lesson.

- Make sure that the service itself involves the active participation of several persons with disabilities.

- If some members of your congregation have experienced the trauma of sudden disability, ask them to share the spiritual journey that went with it. This will help sensitize others to the needs and struggles of those with handicaps.

- If disabled members of your congregation have gone on short-term mission trips, this would be a good time for them to report on their experiences.

- If you have formed a service group to help the disabled, this would be the right time to recruit volunteers.

- Offer a Saturday or Sunday afternoon seminar for those who would like to become more involved in the world of people with disabilities.

92. Resources for Helping the Disabled

ORGANIZATIONS

JAF MINISTRIES

P.O. Box 3333
Agoura Hills, CA 91301
(800) 523-5777

Without question, the best place to learn about ministry with the disabled is JAF Ministries (formerly Joni And Friends). They have developed the most complete set of Christian resources regarding disability. Many helpful tools are available, including a booklet series aimed at handicapped people and a six-week course entitled the *Disability Awareness Study Guide*. They also have a special seminar called the *Christian Institute on Disability,* which could be conducted at your church. In addition, several books written by Joni are listed on the next page.

L'ARCHE

1701 James St.
Syracuse, NY 13206
This is another helpful organization. They
are a Christian-operated residential program
for people with severe disabilities. They are
located in several areas throughout the
United States and Canada. One of their
members, Henri Nouwen, has written a
thought-provoking book regarding disability entitled *In the Name of Jesus* (Crossway
Books, 1989).

BOOKS

All God's Children: Ministry to the Disabled
by Joni Eareckson Tada (Zondervan, 1987).
*Friendship Unlimited: How You Can Help a
Disabled Friend* by Joni Eareckson Tada
and Bev Singleton (Harold Shaw, 1987).
Joni by Joni Eareckson (Zondervan, 1984).

XIII.
LIFE

Championing the Gift of Humanity

As we come to the last section of the book, we hope you have found this collection of ideas and resources to be a helpful boost as you lead your church deeper into the pain of society. We believe in the Church as God's special agent of love. The community of faith is the place where the very idea of forgiveness, charity and hope are lived out. We, bonded together, are the gospel for the world today, the Body of Christ in living action. Could there be anything better for the world? We don't think so.

If we were to sum up the spirit of this book, we would say it is all about *life*: "The thief comes only to steal and kill and destroy," Jesus said. "I have come that they may have life, and have it to the full" (John 10:10). What the Church has to offer to the world is the fullness of life. We are a sanctuary, a place of healing and warmth, a base of courage and vision that compels its members to live in the cauldron of human misery. The people of God give hope to the hopeless, pointing to a day when Christ shall wipe away every last tear.

If this does not excite you, you need to experience the Resurrection!

We have a dream of a Church that feeds the hungry, that clothes the naked, that gives a cup of water to the thirsty, that visits the sick and the prisoner, that cares for the orphan and the widow. We have this vision of a Church that cares for the baby in the womb, the child in the Third World ghetto, the elderly in the convalescent center and the hurting person inside each of our hearts. We have this idea of a Church that advocates on behalf of the oppressed, that dispenses tenderness to the downtrodden, that confronts cruel dictators and landlords. We have this notion of a community of believers where the idea of brokenness, forgiveness, honor and dignity are not doctrines—rather, they are a way of life.

Have we left our senses? No, we think we have found them. And we believe you have, too. We have all imbibed the wine of Christ's Calvary love, and we are now alive to the vision of the Kingdom and its unfathomable offer of life to all God's children.

We know the world longs for this kind of Jesus, for this kind of flesh-and-blood Body of believers.

How will the world know the Messiah has come? Will they hear it in our carefully crafted doctrinal statements, our ecclesiastical rules or our order of service? The prophet Isaiah gives us a clue:

> Is not this the kind of fasting I have chosen: to loose the chains of injustice and untie the cords of the yoke, to set the oppressed free and break every yoke? Is it not to share your food with the hungry and to provide the poor wanderer with shelter—when you see the naked, to clothe him, and not to turn away from your own flesh and blood? *Then your light will break forth like the dawn, and your healing will quickly appear; then your righteousness will go before you, and the glory of the Lord will be your rear guard* (Isa. 58:6-8, emphasis added).

The light of the world. It is seen through the visible acts of God's representatives, His children. This is the life that we bring to the world. This is the high calling of the Church today.

93. Celebrate Life

The idea of tithing in the Old Testament does not exactly fit our contemporary bang-'em-on-the-head-to-get-more-bucks model. Back then, tithing was not linked to a building program, utilities or payroll. It was a system that subsidized a party—a great festival honoring Yahweh's goodness, grace and forgiveness. It was a celebration that He remembered the people's sins no more and dealt with them mercifully.

The Israelites would make their sojourn to the Temple and spend days camping out with family and friends, feasting, drinking, dancing, singing and laughing. Smoke rose to the heavens as the firstfruits were sacrificed in thanksgiving to the Lord. The pyre of death was the altar of life, and all of it went to the Lord. (Caring for the physical needs of others came from the coffers *beyond* the 10 percent.)

Sadly, the Church has lost its party spirit. We have lost the celebration of life. We think the Church could learn a few things from the Israelites of old. Here are a couple of ideas:

- Plan some annual events around the theme of fun. For example, why not let New Year's Eve be a night of enjoyment, rather than a somber time of setting goals (which we all break within the first month anyway)? Have the different age groups decide what would be fun for them, and accommodate the variety of interests. Some may go for a blowout video session of five movies in a row, others may go for stargazing or dinner on the beach.

- Consider ways to provide refreshment and fun to the neighborhood. One church that is located in a residential community has an annual block party. One Saturday a year they block off both ends of the street with barricades and let loose. It is an all-day mix of arts, crafts, games, barbecues and live music provided by musicians from the church and neighborhood.

94. Reclaim the Beauty

In the introduction to the section on the environment, we spoke of the creativity of God. We worship the ultimate artist.

Unfortunately, much of our church life and activism reflects a stoic, bland view of our Creator. Our "art" is limited to a cross above the pulpit, a few prefabricated stained glass windows and a picture of Jesus. Our sense of color is limited to a mix of white walls and red pew cushions.

We are not advocating an extravagant and costly remake of the building. That would be dishonest art—relegating the creative to the wealthy. Most art comes from the stuff of life, the balance of being filled with the glory of God and living like the son of a carpenter. Bringing beauty into our churches requires just a little resolve and a bit of a free spirit. Here are a few suggestions to get you going:

- Find out if any art students are part of your congregation. If so, ask them to provide a sculpture or set of paintings for the vestibule. Encourage them to move beyond traditional categories—something you would not expect to see in a church foyer.

- See if some artists, designers and interior decorators would take a tour of the facilities and suggest ways to bring in more beauty and pizzazz. A fresh landscaping of the garden (plus the addition of a sculpture), a colorful series of wall hangings or new, bright paint can go a long way toward upgrading the surroundings.

- If the climate in your area is conducive, ask the "green thumbs" in your congregation to create a cut flower garden on the premises. A generous supply of fresh flowers throughout the building brings in the living art of our Creator each week.

- Look for musicians to provide a variety of music. The Lord has created all kinds of wonderful sounds and rhythms, and we starve ourselves by staying in a rut.

- Ask your more literary members to create alternative ways to do Scripture readings. Perhaps they could dramatize the text or augment them with contemporary poetry.

95. Be Completely Pro-life

We have heard it said, "When Mother Teresa speaks, everybody listens." What is it about her that she can enter a circle of pro-choice people and have a reasonable conversation, explaining her convictions regarding the injustice of abortion? She does not suffer the usual barrage of criticisms aimed at most "religious fanatics." Her voice is not drowned out by the antagonistic accusations that she is anti women's rights and old-fashioned. Why is that?

Integrity has its own power.

Long before Mother Teresa ever opened her mouth, she lived her life. The world came to conclude she is a saint because of her lifestyle, because of her obvious sacrificial spirit and love for those who are oppressed. She probably believes in the "rights" of human beings more than any other living person we know. And when she speaks of her love for the child in the womb, she backs it up by loving those that society abandons on the other side of the womb.

That is what it means to be completely pro-life—caring for the vulnerable unborn *and* the vulnerable who have been born. We believe the world will not be able to hear the morals that drive our pro-life message until we live moral lives. We must be the people who give to the poor, feed the hungry and give shelter to the homeless. We must be a community of faith that feels no disjunction in teaching English to immigrants, holding hands with friends who have AIDS, pushing for fair housing regulations, opposing racist practices in local business and advocating for unborn rights. We *should* feel the disjunction of proclaiming our love for the life that we cannot see while ignoring the life that we can see. The Scriptures have something to say about that!

No, we must be the ones who champion *all* of life. We urge you as a leader to always ask the question, "Is our church's pro-life stance a reality in the way we touch all of life, or is it merely a slogan?" The answer to that question could lead to all sorts of new activity.

96. Return to the Parish

We opened this book with the idea that we should leave our churches. We hope that has been a pervasive theme throughout all of our ideas. The church that lives separate from the world has not understood Calvary.

The idea of a "parish" does not fit too many of our churches today. We are more like a supermarket or a mall—a place where people come to choose certain products that meet their desires. By itself, this is not a bad idea; it is a valuable service to Christians who have identified personal felt needs. But the Church is much more than a supermarket. Our calling comes out of the mixed-up business of hearing the call of God and listening to the cry of the world. This intersection best describes the duty of local churches.

Pastors across the nation are rediscovering this mission. They are identifying specific geographical regions and relocating there to become a member of the community. The life of their church grows out of the reality experienced by their neighbors.

These church leaders, then, are asking the hard question, "Is our life together ushering in the kingdom of God to this specific area?" That can be a threatening question, but it is the most on-target question we could ask while planning strategies. The services of these local churches do not emanate from boardrooms that are asking "How many more can we get through the door?" The services are designed in the daily experience of walking with the people, hearing their cries and aspirations, and praying to God for mercy. This is what it means to leave the church and live in the parish. If you would like some partnership in implementing a parish ministry, contact Christian Community Development Association (listed in the resource section).

97. Go for Life

We think that as a Christian leader you should regularly nurture your understanding of life in the world. The Scriptures describe Jesus as a man who was acquainted with sorrow (see Isa. 53:3). We do not think that just meant His own afflictions. Jesus' life was marked by a genuine compassion for those who suffered (see Matt. 8:17). Pastors are called to a lifestyle that takes them into a deeper sense of the world's suffering.

As you lead your church, you need to lead with a hand that reaches out to a starving child, a prisoner, a person with AIDS, a woman who just lost her spouse to cancer, a child who lost his innocence to abuse.

Our suggestion is simple enough. If finances allow, we think it should be part of your regular annual routine to travel to parts of the world that can be your classroom in human pain. Over the years, you may want to expose yourself to different places and experiences. Seeing a variety of needs will keep your heart soft and focused on Jesus' call to minister to the "least of these." Church life, with all of its mundane demands and saccharine exploits, can be the most dangerous place for our hearts. We become deluded by the pace of our religious functions, thinking that is the measure of our life in the world. All the while, we are confined to the walls of our sanctuary.

If you need help taking a regular plunge into another culture or country, contact any of the organizations we have listed throughout this book. Or write GlobaLink, which is an executive service for pastors and Christian leaders who want to experience other lands.

98. Give to Life

We have a mystical relationship to blood. Literature of old tries to explain the elements of this liquid and how it gives us life, feeds our personalities and accounts for our spiritual selves. Some of this reading is fascinating, some of it truly bizarre. All of it, however, lifts the lid on the ongoing human need to connect with the source of life.

In the Church, we go much deeper into that mystery. We *do* believe that blood gives us life. We celebrate the blood of Jesus. Through it we have received the forgiveness of sins. Through it we have the gift of eternal life in heaven, where we will enjoy all the benefits of life in its most extravagant and pleasurable forms forever and ever. "No eye has seen, no ear has heard, no mind has conceived what God has prepared for those who love him" (1 Cor. 2:9). All this because of the blood of Jesus.

This is our suggestion: We think churches should organize an annual blood-bank drive. Some in your congregation will be prevented from donating their blood, but the majority will be able to participate. The physical act of giving your blood is a statement of unity with the cross of Christ and equality with the human race; it is a deed that makes you vulnerable to pain because you care about others' pain. It is a form of giving that literally comes from within. Being pro-life does not get much more poetic than this.

99. Spread the Vision for Life

Choose a day on your church's annual calendar to celebrate life. This could be the most complete statement you choose to make that you are inseparably linked to each other and the world. It is the grand statement of love and pain and joy and defeat and hope all mixed together. Here are a few items that could be part of the day:

- Plan the Sunday service around the theme of life and the church's call to live smack in the middle of it.

- Ask your Sunday School teachers to do the same for their lessons that week.

- Recruit your artists, musicians and poets to help design the service and sanctuary around the theme of life.

- Commit a good part of the service to praying for the world in its diverse collection of needs. You could have several adult groups prepare ahead of time to lead the church through different avenues of human pain.

- Be specific about your own community. Try to get a clear profile of the local challenges. As you paint this picture for the congregation, lead them through a time of small-group prayer. Call on the church to ask God for help to live out the gospel in all its fullness in the local community.

- Offer a special Saturday or Sunday afternoon seminar for people who would like to go deeper into the pain of society.

100. Resources for Affirming Life

We have offered more than a hundred first-rate resources throughout this book. All of them will be valuable to you as you live out the full life of the Church. Here we offer a final set that will serve as excellent general resources as you lead your church into all the world.

ORGANIZATIONS

CHRISTIAN COMMUNITY DEVELOPMENT ASSOCIATION (CCDA)
3848 W. Ogden Ave.
Chicago, IL 60623

FEMINISTS FOR LIFE
811 E. 47th St.
Kansas City, MO 64110

GLOBALINK
P.O. Box 25
Colfax, WA 99111

NATIONAL RIGHT TO LIFE COMMITTEE
419 7th St. NW, Suite 500
Washington, DC 20004

BOOKS

Completely Pro-Life by Ron Sider
(InterVarsity, 1987).
Fifty Ways You Can Reach the World by
Tony Campolo and Gordon Aeschliman
(InterVarsity, 1993).
Out of the Saltshaker by Becky Pippert
(InterVarsity, 1979).
Roaring Lambs by Bob Briner
(Zondervan, 1993).
The Body by Chuck Colson, (Word, 1993).
The Global Issues Study Series (InterVarsity,
1989)—12 booklets in all.
When Is It Right to Die? by Joni Eareckson
Tada (Zondervan, 1992).

MAGAZINES

PRISM
10 Lancaster Ave.
Wynnewood, PA 19096

JustLife News
P.O. Box 7165
Grand Rapids, MI 49510

101. Explore God's Word

How to Use This Material for Sunday School, Small Group and Individual Study

As our final idea to you in this book, we offer 13 Sunday School lessons. We have set them up to follow the 13 sections of this book. We have intentionally structured the book around a typical church quarter. That allows this curriculum to slip into the regular set of options you would offer members in any given church quarter.

You may teach the lessons in seven sessions. During the first session, discuss introductory information and one section. For the following sessions, cover two sections. Be sensitive to the needs and interests of your group to know which sections should be given the most attention and which ones could be touched on more lightly in your discussions.

You may also pick and choose a specific session from this curriculum to fit a theme you are emphasizing on any given Sunday. If you have already read the book, you will know that we suggested you influence your church for involvement in world need by devoting an entire Sunday to a specific theme or need. If you choose to do that, you could ask your Sunday School teachers to use the lessons in this section to correspond with your theme.

Each session can be greatly enhanced by a member of your church or a guest who can speak from personal experience. If the session is on "The Poor," for example, try to find someone who has lived in those circumstances. Whenever possible, use someone in your church. This helps prevent the idea that we are doing things for people "out there." Instead, you are left with the sense that you are all a part of the same Body. The success of this portion of the session is dependent on your ability to find someone who can "flesh" out the concept. Your group members may be an excellent resource to help you find these presenters. Show them the list of subjects during the first session and ask them to help you with leads.

Each session has the same basic format and lasts approximately 50 minutes. This is how it flows:

1. **Getting Started** (5 minutes)
2. **Exploring the Word** (10 minutes)
3. **Special Guest** (10 minutes)
4. **Reflection on the Christian's Responsibility** (10 minutes)
5. **Personal Application** (5 minutes)
6. **Further Action Ideas** (5 minutes)
7. **Looking Ahead** (5 minutes)

The following general guidelines will help you organize and conduct the sessions. Keep in mind that the optimum-size discussion group is 10 to 15 people. A smaller group may lose interest unless everyone has a high level of commitment. A larger group will require strong leadership skills to help everyone participate meaningfully.

1. If you are leading a group that already meets regularly, such as a Sunday School class or Bible study group, decide how many weeks to spend on the series and set your dates.

Consider holidays or other events that might affect continuity of attendance. In most cases, 7 to 13 sessions is a good time length to adequately deal with the major issues in the book.

2. If you want to start a Bible study or Christian service group, enlist two or three people as a nucleus for the group. Work with these participants to determine the meeting time, dates and place that are best for your group and involve them in inviting other people to participate.

Encourage people to register their intention to attend, both to help you in planning and to raise their determination to be there.

Follow up with reminder phone calls.

3. Arrange for quality child care for each session.

4. Plan for light refreshments to be served each session as people arrive to encourage a climate of friendly interchange.

5. Arrange seating informally, either in one semicircle or several smaller circles of no more than eight chairs per circle.

6. At the first session, provide a copy of the book for each participant and a typed schedule for the series. In most cases, people will put more into the series—both at home and at the sessions—if they buy the book themselves.

7. Briefly share one or two personal ways this book has challenged and motivated you, the leader. This sharing should not be a sales pitch for the book.

Demonstrate honest sharing, being open with the group about your own desire to live out your commitment to Christ. As discussion leader, you need not be the "expert." The group will appreciate your being a fellow-learner.

Sharing insights and experiences is a good approach to beginning any of the sessions of the series. As the series progresses and participants become comfortable with one another, open some sessions by inviting participants to share one step they have taken to "change the world" since the last session.

8. In each session, lead participants in discussing the listed questions. If you have more than 8 or 10 people in your group, assign some of the questions to be discussed in smaller groups, then invite each group to share one or two insights with the larger group.

Alternate large-group and small-group discussion to provide variety and to allow every participant a comfortable option in which to contribute. Try various combinations in forming small groups: groups based on Christian service experience, separate groups for men and women, groups based on geographical location within the community and so on.

9. In guiding the discussions, the following tips are helpful:

- If a question or comment is raised that is off the subject, either suggest that it be dealt with at another time or ask the group if they would prefer to pursue the new issue now.

- If someone talks too much, direct a few questions specifically to other people, making sure not to put a shy person on the spot. Talk privately with the "dominator," asking for his or her cooperation in helping to draw out a few of the quieter participants.

- If someone does not participate verbally, assign a few questions to be discussed in pairs, trios or other small groups. Or, distribute paper and pencils and ask people to write their answer to a specific question or two. Then invite several people, including the "shy" one, to read what they wrote.

- If someone asks a question and you do not know the answer, admit it and move on. If the question calls for insight about personal experience, invite participants to comment.

If the question requires specialized knowledge, offer to look for an answer in the library, from your pastor or from some other appropriate resource before the next session.

10. Pray regularly for the sessions and the participants. As you guide people in learning from God's Word, He will honor your service and bring rich benefits into the lives of those who participate.

Evangelism

BIBLICAL BASIS: JONAH 1-4

GETTING STARTED (5 MINUTES)
Before the session, record section I, "Evangelism," starting at "A song many of us" and ending at "we cannot temporarily breathe" on a cassette recorder. Begin the session by playing the tape recording. Ask, **What responses does "the tension of not being at home while at the same time being at home" elicit in most Christians?**

EXPLORING THE WORD (10 MINUTES)
Overview of Jonah 1-4
    I. Jonah is disobedient—Jonah 1:1-11
    II. Jonah is swallowed by the fish—Jonah 1:12—2:10
    III. The Ninevites repent—Jonah 3
    IV. God is compassionate—Jonah 4

Divide members into four groups. Assign to each group one of the four Scripture passages (Jonah 1:1-11; 1:12-2:10; 3; 4). Have each group read the passage and summarize Jonah's actions and God's actions and the results. Allow groups to record and share their findings.

SPECIAL GUEST (10 MINUTES)

Introduce your guest. We suggest you invite someone who recently became a Christian.

REFLECTION ON THE CHRISTIAN'S RESPONSIBILITY (10 MINUTES)

Discuss the following questions.

1. To what extent are we responsible to and for the unsaved?
2. How do the evangelism efforts you are aware of convey or not convey the concern God has for the unsaved?
3. How might we be insulating ourselves from those outside the family of faith?

PERSONAL APPLICATION (5 MINUTES)

Take a few moments of silence to think through some ways God is nudging you to move out of your Christian ghetto and into the world. Write them down. Share them with a group member.

FURTHER ACTION IDEAS (5 MINUTES)

Consider "Ways 1-8" in section I, "Evangelism." As a group, think of how your church could be better evangelists of the good news.

LOOKING AHEAD (5 MINUTES)

Ask group members to read section II, "The Poor" and/or Genesis 41:41-57 before the next session. Close with group prayer for God's movement and your action in the area of evangelism.

SESSION 2

The Poor

BIBLICAL BASIS: GENESIS 41:41-57

GETTING STARTED (5 MINUTES)
Begin by asking, **What unique role do the poor play in our society?**

EXPLORING THE WORD (10 MINUTES)
Overview of Genesis 41:41-57
 I. Joseph is given charge of Egypt—Genesis 41:41-45
 II. Joseph and Egypt are prosperous—Genesis 41:46-52
 III. Famine in the land—Genesis 41:53-55
 IV. Joseph provides food—Genesis 41:56,57

Ask a group member to read aloud the Scripture passage. As a group, outline the events of this passage. Say, **Through a dream, God told Joseph of the coming famine. What options were there for Egypt's prosperity? What responsibility did Joseph have? To whom?**

SPECIAL GUEST (10 MINUTES)

Introduce your guest. We suggest you invite someone who has lived in poverty.

REFLECTION ON THE CHRISTIAN'S RESPONSIBILITY (10 MINUTES)

Discuss the following questions.

1. In what different ways does poverty express itself today?
2. What do you think are the key causes of poverty? What can be done to rectify these problems?
3. Beyond providing for material needs, how can the Church minister to poor people?

PERSONAL APPLICATION (5 MINUTES)

Take a few moments of silence to think through some ways God is nudging you to involve your life with poor people. Write them down. Share them with a group member.

FURTHER ACTION IDEAS (5 MINUTES)

Consider "Ways 9-16" in section II, "The Poor." As a group, think of how your church could minister to poor people.

LOOKING AHEAD (5 MINUTES)

Ask group members to read section III, "Youth" and/or 1 Samuel 3:1-18 before the next session. Close with group prayer for God's movement and your action among poor people.

Youth

BIBLICAL BASIS: 1 SAMUEL 3:1-18

GETTING STARTED (5 MINUTES)
Begin by dividing your group into pairs. Ask, **At the age of 10, what was most important to you? Who influenced you?**

EXPLORING THE WORD (10 MINUTES)
Overview of 1 Samuel 3:1-18
   I. Samuel ministers in the Temple—1 Samuel 3:1,2
  II. God calls Samuel—1 Samuel 3:3-8
 III. Eli instructs Samuel—1 Samuel 3:9
 IV. Samuel listens to God—1 Samuel 3:10-14
  V. Samuel delivers God's message—1 Samuel 3:15-18

Have group members remain in pairs and read the Scripture passage. Ask, **How did God work through Samuel? What caused Samuel to listen to God?** As a group, list the ways adults influence youth.

SPECIAL GUEST (10 MINUTES)
Introduce your guest. We suggest a youth
from your church.

REFLECTION ON THE CHRISTIAN'S RESPONSIBILITY (10 MINUTES)
Discuss the following questions.
1. What special challenges do youth bring to the
   Church today? How can the Church meet these
   challenges?
2. What can the Church do to bridge itself to
   youth?
3. What unique role can parents play in ministering to their children and to others' children?

PERSONAL APPLICATION (5 MINUTES)
Take a few moments of silence to think through some
ways God is nudging you to involve your life with youth.
Write them down. Share them with a group member.

FURTHER ACTION IDEAS (5 MINUTES)
Consider "Ways 17-24" in section III, "Youth." As a group,
think of how your church could minister to youth.

LOOKING AHEAD (5 MINUTES)
Ask group members to read section IV, "Missions"
and/or Acts 13:44-48 before the next session.
Close with group prayer for God's movement and your
action among youth.

Missions

BIBLICAL BASIS: ACTS 13:44-48

GETTING STARTED (5 MINUTES)
Begin by saying, **Do you agree or disagree with the following statement: We are to minister first to those who are around us. Why do you agree or disagree?**

EXPLORING THE WORD (10 MINUTES)
Overview of Acts 13:44-48
  I. The Jews speak against Paul and Barnabas—Acts 13:44,45
  II. The gospel is available to the Gentiles—Acts 13:46,47
  III. The Gentiles respond—Acts 13:48

Read the passage aloud. Say, **God planned for the message of salvation to spread "to the ends of the earth." How did this affect the Jews? The Gentiles?**

SPECIAL GUEST (10 MINUTES)

Introduce your guest. We suggest you invite someone who is a Christian as a result of missions' work.

REFLECTION ON THE CHRISTIAN'S RESPONSIBILITY (10 MINUTES)

Discuss the following questions.

1. What has been the Church's response to the spread of other religions, especially Islam?
2. What are the obstacles that keep people from being involved in missions?
3. What impact does the spread of the gospel world-wide have on the local Church body?

PERSONAL APPLICATION (5 MINUTES)

Take a few moments of silence to think through some ways God is nudging you to move out of your Christian "ghetto" and into the world. Write them down. Share them with a group member.

FURTHER ACTION IDEAS (5 MINUTES)

Consider "Ways 25-32" in section IV, "Missions." As a group, think of how your church could minister in the area of missions.

LOOKING AHEAD (5 MINUTES)

Ask group members to read section V, "The Environment" and/or Genesis 2:4-15 and Leviticus 25:3-12 before the next session. Close with group prayer for God's movement and your action in the area of missions.

The Environment

BIBLICAL BASIS: GENESIS 1:27-31; 2:4-15;
LEVITICUS 25:3-12

GETTING STARTED (5 MINUTES)
Begin by saying, **Picture a beautiful, scenic location
you have visited. Consider the different elements
of this place. What does this scenic location tell you
about God?**

EXPLORING THE WORD (10 MINUTES)
Overview of Genesis 1:27-31; 2:4-15
  I. God creates us—Genesis 1:27; 2:4-7
 II. God's garden described—Genesis 2:8-14
III. We are given responsibility for the garden—
      Genesis 1:28; 2:15

Overview of Leviticus 25:3-12
  I. Instructions to work the land—Leviticus 25:3
 II. Sabbath year of rest for the land—Leviticus 25:4-7
III. Year of jubilee for the land—Leviticus 25:8-12

Divide group members into two groups. Have one group
read Genesis 1:27-31 and 2:4-15 and list God's purpose
in creating us. Also, list our responsibilities. Have the
other group read Leviticus 25:3-12 and list the results of
the sabbath year and year of jubilee on the land. Allow
groups to share findings.

SPECIAL GUEST (10 MINUTES)

Introduce your guest. We suggest you invite a nonprofessional environmentalist.

REFLECTION ON THE CHRISTIAN'S RESPONSIBILITY (10 MINUTES)

Discuss the following questions.

1. What impact can the local church have on environments outside its geographical location?
2. How does our call to care for creation coincide with and differ from other environmental movements?
3. Why do you think the Church has been slow to become involved in the care of creation?

PERSONAL APPLICATION (5 MINUTES)

Take a few moments of silence to think through some ways God is nudging you to be involved with the environment. Write them down. Share them with a group member.

FURTHER ACTION IDEAS (5 MINUTES)

Consider "Ways 33-40" in section V, "The Environment." As a group, think of how your church could be better stewards of God's creation.

LOOKING AHEAD (5 MINUTES)

Ask group members to read section VI, "The Sick" and/or Mark 10:46-52 before the next session. Close with group prayer for God's movement and your action in the area of the environment.

The Sick

BIBLICAL BASIS: MARK 10:46-52

GETTING STARTED (5 MINUTES)
Begin by reading from some magazines and/or newspapers on the issue of health care. Ask, **What important issues for a sick person do these neglect to address?**

EXPLORING THE WORD (10 MINUTES)
Overview of Mark 10:46-52
  I. Bartimaeus calls to Jesus—Mark 10:46,47
  II. Jesus responds—Mark 10:48-50
  III. Bartimaeus requests healing—Mark 10:51
  IV. Jesus heals Bartimaeus—Mark 10:52

Divide group members into groups of two or three. Have members read the passage. Ask, **How do you think Bartimaeus felt at each point in the account?** Allow them to share their findings.

SPECIAL GUEST (10 MINUTES)
Introduce your guest. We suggest you invite someone who has experienced a long-term illness or a family member of such a person.

REFLECTION ON THE CHRISTIAN'S RESPONSIBILITY (10 MINUTES)
Discuss the following questions.
1. In the past, the Church was a leader in caring for the sick. What has caused a change in this?
2. What responsibility do we have to the mentally disabled?
3. How might we be insulating ourselves from those who are sick?

PERSONAL APPLICATION (5 MINUTES)
Take a few moments of silence to think through some ways God is nudging you to be involved with sick people. Write them down. Share them with a group member.

FURTHER ACTION IDEAS (5 MINUTES)
Consider "Ways 41-47" in section VI, "The Sick." As a group, think of how your church could minister to the sick.

LOOKING AHEAD (5 MINUTES)
Ask group members to read section VII, "Prisoners" and/or Acts 16:16-40 before the next session. Close with group prayer for God's movement and your action among sick people.

Prisoners

BIBLICAL BASIS: ACTS 16:16-40

GETTING STARTED (5 MINUTES)
Begin by asking, **What are the titles of some films or books that portray prison life? What do they communicate about prisoners?**

EXPLORING THE WORD (10 MINUTES)
Overview of Acts 16:16-40
 I. Claims are made against Paul and Silas—
   Acts 16:16-21
 II. Paul and Silas are beaten and imprisoned—
   Acts 16:22-24
 III. An earthquake releases Paul and Silas—Acts 16:25-30
 IV. The jailer and his family are baptized—Acts 16:31-34
 V. Paul requests justice—Acts 16:35-40

Ask a group member to read aloud the Scripture passage. As a group, outline the actions and attitude of the jailer toward Paul and Silas. Ask, **What caused this change in the jailer?**

SPECIAL GUEST (10 MINUTES)

Introduce your guest. We suggest you invite someone who has been imprisoned or a family member of such a person.

REFLECTION ON THE CHRISTIAN'S RESPONSIBILITY (10 MINUTES)

Discuss the following questions.

1. What challenges are unique to a ministry to prisoners?
2. How can we remove the stigma of having a loved one in prison?
3. What can be done to keep in mind the needs of prisoners who are out of our sight?

PERSONAL APPLICATION (5 MINUTES)

Take a few moments of silence to think through some ways God is nudging you to be involved with prisoners. Write them down. Share them with a group member.

FURTHER ACTION IDEAS (5 MINUTES)

Consider "Ways 48-55" in section VII, "Prisoners." As a group, think of how your church could minister to prisoners.

LOOKING AHEAD (5 MINUTES)

Ask group members to read section VIII, "The Elderly" and/or Joshua 14:6-14 before the next session. Close with group prayer for God's movement and your action among prisoners.

The Elderly

BIBLICAL BASIS: JOSHUA 14:6-14

GETTING STARTED (5 MINUTES)
Begin by showing a picture of an elderly person. Say,
**What one word comes to mind when you look at
this picture?** Have each person respond. Repeat with
other pictures.

EXPLORING THE WORD (10 MINUTES)
Overview of Joshua 14:6-14
 I. Caleb reminds Joshua of the past—Joshua 14:6-9
 II. Caleb declares his competence—Joshua 14:10,11
III. Caleb requests his promised land—Joshua 14:12
IV. Joshua blesses and rewards Caleb—Joshua 14:13,14

Divide group members into pairs. Have pairs
read the Scripture passage and write a description
(physical, emotional, intellectual) of Caleb. Have
group members share findings.

SPECIAL GUEST (10 MINUTES)

Introduce your guest. We suggest you invite an elderly person from your church.

REFLECTION ON THE CHRISTIAN'S RESPONSIBILITY (10 MINUTES)

Discuss the following questions.

1. What are some of the greatest concerns of elderly people?
2. How might we be insulating ourselves from the elderly?
3. What special benefits are there in ministering to the elderly?

PERSONAL APPLICATION (5 MINUTES)

Take a few moments of silence to think through some ways God is nudging you to be involved with elderly people. Write them down. Share them with a group member.

FURTHER ACTION IDEAS (5 MINUTES)

Consider "Ways 56-62" in section VIII, "The Elderly." As a group, think of how your church could minister to elderly people.

LOOKING AHEAD (5 MINUTES)

Ask group members to read section IX, "The Immigrant" and/or Matthew 2:13-16 before the next session. Close with group prayer for God's movement and your action among elderly people.

The Immigrant

BIBLICAL BASIS: MATTHEW 2:13-16

GETTING STARTED (5 MINUTES)
Begin by saying, **Personal tragedy has caused you to relocate to another country. You don't know the language or people or customs. Your finances are limited and contact with home is improbable. What do you do?**

EXPLORING THE WORD (10 MINUTES)
Overview of Matthew 2:13-16
  I. Joseph is instructed to leave Israel—Matthew 2:13
 II. Joseph, Mary and Jesus flee to Egypt—Matthew 2:14,15
III. Herod tries to have Jesus killed—Matthew 2:16

Have a group member read aloud the Scripture passage. Say, **Joseph and Mary were Jews who had lived all their lives in Israel. Israel was home to their families and the only land they knew. Ask, What do you think Mary and Joseph thought and felt as they fled to Egypt? What obstacles did they probably face once they were in Egypt?**

SPECIAL GUEST (10 MINUTES)

Introduce your guest. We suggest you invite someone who is a recent immigrant to this country.

REFLECTION ON THE CHRISTIAN'S RESPONSIBILITY (10 MINUTES)

Discuss the following questions.

1. To what extent are we responsible to and for the immigrant?
2. What special efforts can the Church take on to convey God's love for the immigrant?
3. How might we be insulating ourselves from immigrants?

PERSONAL APPLICATION (5 MINUTES)

Take a few moments of silence to think through some ways God is nudging you to be involved with immigrants. Write them down. Share them with a group member.

FURTHER ACTION IDEAS (5 MINUTES)

Consider "Ways 63-70" in section IX, "The Immigrant." As a group, think of how your church could minister to immigrants.

LOOKING AHEAD (5 MINUTES)

Ask group members to read section X, "The Family" and/or Ruth 1:1—2:3 before the next session. Close with group prayer for God's movement and your action among immigrants.

SESSION 10

The Family

BIBLICAL BASIS: RUTH 1:1–2:3

GETTING STARTED (5 MINUTES)
Begin by asking a group member to read aloud from section X, "The Family," starting at "It seems America" and ending at "not a pretty picture." Ask, **What do you think of these statements?**

EXPLORING THE WORD (10 MINUTES)
Overview of Ruth 1:1—2:3
  I. Naomi loses her husband and sons—Ruth 1:1-5
 II. Ruth stays with Naomi—Ruth 1:6-18
III. Ruth and Naomi return to Bethlehem—Ruth 1:19-22
IV. Ruth works for Naomi and herself—Ruth 2:1-3

Divide group members into groups of two or three. Have them read the scripture passage and discuss the following questions: **What hardships did Ruth and Naomi have to overcome? What were Ruth's obligations to her mother-in-law? What caused Ruth to act as she did?**

SPECIAL GUEST (10 MINUTES)

Introduce your guest. We suggest you invite someone who lives in a unique family environment.

REFLECTION ON THE CHRISTIAN'S RESPONSIBILITY (10 MINUTES)

Discuss the following questions.

1. What special role does the family play in the spiritual growth of the individual?
2. How do we respond to the needs of nontraditional families while still promoting the traditional family?
3. How is your family an avenue of ministry for you?

PERSONAL APPLICATION (5 MINUTES)

Take a few moments of silence to think through some ways God is nudging you to be involved with families. Write them down. Share them with a group member.

FURTHER ACTION IDEAS (5 MINUTES)

Consider "Ways 71-78" in section X, "The Family." As a group, think of how your church could minister to families.

LOOKING AHEAD (5 MINUTES)

Ask group members to read section XI, "The Oppressed" and/or Exodus 1:8-16 before the next session. Close with group prayer for God's movement and your action among families.

The Oppressed

BIBLICAL BASIS: EXODUS 1:8-16

GETTING STARTED (5 MINUTES)
Begin by having each group member complete the following statement: **Oppression is....**

EXPLORING THE WORD (10 MINUTES)
Overview of Exodus 1:8-16
  I. A new king comes to rule—Exodus 1:8-10
 II. The Israelites are oppressed into slavery—
     Exodus 1:11
III. The oppression is increased—Exodus 1:12-14
 IV. The king tries to have Jewish boys killed—
     Exodus 1:15,16

Have a group member read aloud the Scripture passage.
Have group members list the changes that would have
occurred in the life (work, family, religious practice, etc.)
of the average Israelite as a result of the oppression.

SPECIAL GUEST (10 MINUTES)

Introduce your guest. We suggest you invite someone who has lived in an oppressive situation.

REFLECTION ON THE CHRISTIAN'S RESPONSIBILITY (10 MINUTES)

Discuss the following questions.

1. What unique role can a Christian who is in an oppressive situation play in bringing about justice?
2. In working toward justice, how should the actions of a Christian differ from those of a non-Christian?
3. Think of an oppressive situation that is beyond the immediate influence of your group. What action can be taken in this situation?

PERSONAL APPLICATION (5 MINUTES)

Take a few moments of silence to think through some ways God is nudging you to be involved with oppressed people. Write them down. Share them with a group member.

FURTHER ACTION IDEAS (5 MINUTES)

Consider "Ways 79-85" in section XI, "The Oppressed." As a group, think of how your church could minister to oppressed people.

LOOKING AHEAD (5 MINUTES)

Ask group members to read section XII, "The Disabled" and/or 2 Samuel 9:1-13 before the next session. Close with group prayer for God's movement and your action among oppressed people.

The Disabled

BIBLICAL BASIS: 2 SAMUEL 9:1-13

GETTING STARTED (5 MINUTES)
Begin by saying, **Draw a symbol to represent a disability.** Have group members share their drawings.

EXPLORING THE WORD (10 MINUTES)
Overview of 2 Samuel 9:1-13
  I. David learns of Mephibosheth—2 Samuel 9:1-4
 II. David pledges to care for Mephibosheth—2 Samuel 9:5-8
III. Ziba is ordered to work for Mephibosheth—2 Samuel 9:9,10
IV. Mephibosheth lives with David—2 Samuel 9:11-13

Ask, **What do you think was the plight of a disabled person during Old Testament times?** Divide group members into pairs. Have them read the Scripture passage and ask, **What opportunities did David provide for Mephibosheth?** Have pairs share their findings.

SPECIAL GUEST (10 MINUTES)

Introduce your guest. We suggest you invite someone who is disabled.

REFLECTION ON THE CHRISTIAN'S RESPONSIBILITY (10 MINUTES)

Discuss the following questions.

1. To what extent are we responsible to and for the disabled?
2. What can the Church do to show God's special love for the disabled?
3. In what ways do we prevent the disabled from being active participants in our churches?

PERSONAL APPLICATION (5 MINUTES)

Take a few moments of silence to think through some ways God is nudging you to be involved with the disabled. Write them down. Share them with a group member.

FURTHER ACTION IDEAS (5 MINUTES)

Consider "Ways 86-92" in section XII, "The Disabled." As a group, think of how your church could minister to the disabled.

LOOKING AHEAD (5 MINUTES)

Ask group members to read section XIII, "Life" and/or Matthew 11:16-19 before the next session. Close with group prayer for God's movement and your action among the disabled.

Life

BIBLICAL BASIS: MATTHEW 11:16-19;
JOHN 10:10

GETTING STARTED (5 MINUTES)
Begin by dividing group members into pairs. Ask, **What has been your most life-invigorating experience?**

EXPLORING THE WORD (10 MINUTES)
Overview of Matthew 11:16-19
  I. Jesus assesses the people—Matthew 11:16
 II. The people reject every approach—Matthew 11:17
III. Jesus chooses life—Matthew 11:18,19

Ask a group member to read aloud the Scripture passage. Say, **As John the Baptist's approach was appropriate for his ministry, Jesus' approach fulfilled the need of those around Him.** Ask, **What excuses did people use for rejecting Jesus' approach?** Ask a group member to read aloud John 10:10. Ask, **What does "to the full" or "abundantly" mean?**

SPECIAL GUEST (10 MINUTES)
Introduce your guest. We suggest you invite someone who is involved in a life-celebrating or life-promoting ministry.

REFLECTION ON THE CHRISTIAN'S RESPONSIBILITY (10 MINUTES)
Discuss the following questions.
1. What are the most neglected aspects in celebrating and promoting life?
2. What attitudes or patterns of behavior keep the Church from being "completely pro-life"?
3. In what ways can Christians be the leaders in living life "to the fullest"?

PERSONAL APPLICATION (5 MINUTES)
Take a few moments of silence to think through some ways God is nudging you to be involved in celebrating and promoting life. Write them down. Share them with a group member.

FURTHER ACTION IDEAS (5 MINUTES)
Consider "Ways 93-100" in section XIII, "Life." As a group, think of how your church could celebrate and promote life.